The Apostles of Hillcrest High

Karen Tokarse

ISBN-13:978-1721563616

ISBN-10:172156361X

DEDICATION

I dedicate this book to my best friend and husband, Bill Tokarse, who was the inspiration for the character, David. Both are strong, humble and Godly men, who are governed by the Holy Spirit and continually in conversation with our Holy Father and His Only Son, our Lord and Savior Jesus Christ. My husband is one of the finest Christians I've ever met. God has blessed us beyond anything we could have ever imagined. Thank You JESUS!

Contents

PREFACE

1 Corinthians 2:14 – But the natural man receiveth not the things of the Spirit of God: for they are foolishness unto him: neither can he know them, because they are spiritually discerned.

To the unsaved, this book will not be understood – in fact, will be ridiculed and discounted. Jesus tells us to PRAY for those who spitefully use you, so we pray that those eyes will be opened to God's Truth. But to those who are truly following and striving to be more like Jesus every day, this book will bring great knowledge – especially if you're being attacked by the demonic realm or if you're just searching for ways to feel the presence of God and gain a greater understanding of Him.

Before I became aware of the demonic attacks on the children of God, I was fascinated with new age teachings, followed the teachings of Edgar Cayce and most of the books I bought dealt in the supernatural. I know now that I was searching for anything that would fill the void we ALL have – that only the Creator of this universe can fill – The Lord Jesus Christ! God in His Grace, prevented me from going further which I know now would have ended in witchcraft.

1 Timothy 4:1 – Now the Spirit speaketh expressly, that in the latter times some shall depart from the faith, giving heed to seducing spirits, and doctrines of devils;

One day in 2008 (a pivotal year of awakening for the body of Christ), I fell in our dock. I love the water, but I cannot swim. Consequently, I always wore a life jacket when out on the water. Since I was in the dock, I didn't feel the need to put one on. Other times I had fallen, I had been able to get back out.

What I'm about to tell you is the truth. I don't care if people believe me or not. All I know is that my life changed drastically after that day, so much so, that I don't even feel like the same person.

If you had asked me a minute before the fall that if I died, would I go to heaven? I would have said, "Oh yes. I accepted Jesus when I was 13." I said a prayer in my closet, asking Jesus to save me. I know it was real because I cried and felt His Presence. But I had no one to disciple me after that. There was a big, white DUSTY Bible on our coffee table that no one read. In fact, I had never even read the Bible. I tried several times, but it just didn't make sense to me. Nor did I feel it necessary to learn more about Him. I didn't even THINK about Him unless I was in trouble. What kind of relationship is that?

Walking in our double, covered, enclosed dock, as I had done many times before, somehow I stepped wrong and ended up dropping right between two Sea-Doos tied up in one of the bays. Whenever I fall into water like that, fear overtakes me – remembering a time as a child swimming when I went too far into the deep end of the pool. I must have been around six or seven. All I remember is sinking like a rock before a life guard pulled me out of the water. That life guard saved my life. God, please bless and protect that man – wherever he is! That same fear engulfed me again, but I knew I could dog paddle to the top of the water and get out. I had not had time to take a breath of air before I fell, so the time to get to the surface was critical.

Instead of getting closer to the top, I realized with horror that I was being "pulled down" by unseen forces. In the natural, it didn't make sense. There was 28 feet of water under our dock, but I was being pulled down much deeper. While I studied a lot of supernatural things, I never believed in demons – that was Hellyweird stuff – but somehow the knowledge came to me that that's exactly what it was – demons pulling me down. I saw my deck shoe float up and at that moment, realized that I could not even get to that shoe, let alone the top of the water.

Suddenly I was filled with complete terror. There are no words for this kind of fear. Every cell in my body was terrorized because, at that moment, I KNEW I was going to hell. Once saved, always saved is a LIE from the pit of hell! I truly believe that right before someone dies, they know *exactly* where they're going.

With my whole being filled with terror, Jesus appeared right in front of me. He looked so sad because He knew I was going to hell as well. (Somehow I knew His thoughts.) I looked at Him and said, "Jesus, I'm so sorry I didn't live my life for you."

At that SECOND, I was at the top of the water. I coughed and sputtered and stayed there several minutes. I was crying. When I came out of the enclosed dock, I looked up at the sky and I could not believe how BLUE it was! I couldn't believe how green the trees were! When did that happen? All the colors were more vivid than I'd ever seen. I thought lack of oxygen in my brain may have caused this, but it was a good thing because everything was so much more beautiful! I have since learned that when Muslims and other cult religions accept Jesus – I mean *really* accept Jesus, many have the same experiences with enhanced colors. It's almost like a gray mist or a demonic presence leaves. Hallelujah!

I later discovered that I could pick up my Bible and read it and understand it. I am a voracious reader and had tried to read the Bible several times before, but it was too hard. Now, supernaturally, I could understand it. Plus, I started remembering and REPENTING for all my sins. I felt deep in my heart all the things I did that must have hurt my Father and Jesus. I've never been much of a crier, but I must have cried for two solid years. I needed that cleansing and God was faithful. Even now something will come to mind that I had completely forgotten about, and I will ask Him to forgive me. Then I forgive myself.

I started to go back to church, but quickly discovered that something wasn't right. I wanted to scream that the preaching and teaching were so watered down in comparison to what I had experienced in the water. I wanted to shake women my age. Please WAKE UP! There is so much more to Jesus! I tried to attend Presbyterian (previous denomination), then Baptist. I was just so hungry for more, and these denominations just did not cut it. So I discovered some Pentecostal churches and started attending those. After several years of attending these churches, being filled with the Holy Spirit and walking and talking with our Lord daily, praying one morning, I heard in my spirit: "If you're still sitting under that ministry when I return, you'll be left behind." I realized that a lot of Pentecostal churches are filled with "drama" and not much true praise and worship for the One who died for us.

I learned then that there's something about sitting "under" a church or a "ministry" for which we will be held accountable. We had better make sure the ministry we're sitting under is preaching the true Word and teaching people how to act like Jesus! Just ask God is He wants you somewhere else. He does not want any of us led astray with false teaching – which is so prevalent.

Since coming out of the water, I changed – I mean completely – like night and day. At the same time, my husband, Bill, was having his own encounter with our God and was radically saved as well. One of the first lessons we learned was how to get our mouths in sync with the Word. Jesus said, "You can have what you say." And we were saying what the devil was saying. We started reading the Bible and studying with an incredible hunger for the Word. God blessed that and we have been walking in the supernatural ever since. We did not look back. We both became so dedicated to living for the Will of God, that we cut off our television; we stopped listening to music with demonic beats – including Christian music. We learned how to lay hands on each other for healing. We learned how to anoint us AND our house to rout demonic activity. We've learned how to rebuke storms. In other words, we've learned how to ACT like Jesus in everything we do. *Trust in the Lord with all thine heart and lean not to your own understanding.* We forgive others instantly and we ASK for forgiveness from others. None of us can live in this fallen world and not be affected by satan's agenda.

Because our home is a home of peace and quiet, we are both able to discern any demonic spirit that tries to invade. If you think just because you're going to church once a week you don't have demons, then I encourage you to ask GOD – let Him show you what's really going on in your life.

We've thrown out all rock and roll music, all new age books and paraphernalia from my years of confusion, and I continually ask God to SHOW me if there is anything in my life that displeases Him. Since I know where a lot of people are going if they don't start living for Jesus, I desperately want to tell people to change. Turn to the One who will never leave you nor forsake you. He gave His life for YOU because He loves you. Thank You JESUS!

The entire time I've been writing this book, I've been getting the message, "No one is training my children on how to combat the satanic forces," which is why I've included ways to bind and rebuke evil forces. The weakest Christian can fight the most demonic force coming against them. However, they MUST be committed to our Lord Jesus Christ and *believe* Him when He said *I give you power over ALL the power of the enemy; and nothing shall by any means hurt you.*

I look at the entire witchcraft-driven books with kids dressing up like their favorite characters and emulating their witchcraft skills; I look at the demonic themes of movies; I look at the rock bands covered in satanic attire. All this is used by the evil forces for predictive programming to our most vulnerable – our kids – and parents aren't using discernment of this evil programming. They let their kids wear demonic clothes, put up demonic posters and watch and play demonic movies and recordings – starting with cartoons – which parents use as a babysitter! Imagine that – turning on satanic programming as a babysitter for their kids.

It's common knowledge that most music is taken into a "dedication room" in which the recording is dedicated to satan. Demons enter these recordings, and if someone BUYS these recordings, that gives demons legal rights to attack their prey. Hollywood makes good use of these practices. Most performers have taken a vow to satan and don't think it's all that serious – it's all part of the game for fame. They make witchcraft look cool and Christians look like uninformed and unenlightened imbeciles, when the exact opposite is true. How this must hurt the One Who GAVE HIS LIFE FOR US!

What's really sad is that these books and movies are teaching young kids how to not only dress in witchcraft garb, but how to perform black magic and spells – witchcraft! They think it's a game, but after years of this "practice," they think there is no way out. They realize that their lives have not improved (satan is a liar), but instead has become much worse. They need to realize that JESUS is the way out. There is *nothing* anyone has done that can't be forgiven – even animal and human sacrifices.

It is my wish that our kids will be able to DISCERN the spirits behind any message in books, movies, TV, internet, FRIENDS, etc. that give glory to witchcraft and the demonic realm.

My God. In Him will I trust.

Those of us in deliverance know that all these demons want is your precious soul. Jesus said that *satan has come to steal, kill and destroy, but I have come that they may have life and have it in abundance.* Christians have power over all demons in the name and authority of the Lord Jesus Christ. They don't have to resort to satan's frequency; they can have the REAL POWER – the power of the Lord Jesus Christ!

For we wrestle not against flesh and blood, but against principalities, against powers, against the rulers of the darkness of this world, against spiritual wickedness in high places. *He who is in me is greater than he who is in the world.* Jesus IS that power – The power that He has given to His children. Hallelujah!

1 DAVID JONATHAN EVERETT

It was hard to believe that we were already two months into the senior year. I was determined to stay focused on my goals for the next five years:

1. To graduate without getting involved in ANY dramas (especially female relationships)

2. Graduate Hillcrest High with honors

3. Help my dad with his various missions through the summer and most of the next year

4. Apply to seminary (not sure which one yet)

5. Move to wherever to attend said seminary

6. Graduate fluent in Greek and Hebrew

7. Be hired as a pastor of a small, Spirit-filled church

That shouldn't be too hard. I had the best parents in the world – Rachel and Robert Everett. They had been childhood sweethearts who both loved Jesus, attended college together, became missionaries in Columbia, and moved back to the States so we (my older sister, Beth, and younger sister, Anna, and I) could get an American education. My father was a very strong, principled man who spoke about Jesus to everyone he met, and whose God-given talents were primarily focused on helping others. He had a natural sense between those who really needed help from those who were gaming the system – and guilt-ridden Christians. But he also knew *"the natural man receiveth not the things of the Spirit of God: for they are foolishness unto him: neither can he know them, because they are spiritually discerned."* Some people just wouldn't receive the Gospel no matter how hard you tried. We just prayed for those lost people. He often said he had never met anyone who regretted turning to Jesus. In fact, most people's lives were so dramatically changed, that they expressed regret in waiting so long. I hoped to develop that same sense of discernment.

My father had inherited a literal fortune from his grandfather who had a knack for buying seemingly worthless land in Texas and Louisiana, only to discover later to have been rich in oil and minerals. My grandfather nearly died during a rig explosion, experienced a Damascus road salvation and lived his life for Jesus for the rest of his life. My Dad's parents had died in a plane crash going to one of the oil fields and, as the only heir, inherited my grandfather's vast estate.

Instead of spending the money on himself and his family, he and my mom started a grass-roots ministry helping others and getting other successful business men and women to donate and participate. Many community leaders respected him because he always gave glory to God and took none of the credit for himself. He never accepted accolades, but told the press of an "anonymous benefactor." But most people knew the truth of his benevolence. He also had Christian "help" in politicians, police, fire, rescue, etc.

Both my mom and dad encouraged me to be separate from the crowd; to be a leader for GOD, and I had followed those precepts all my life. If I saw a friend headed in the wrong direction,

I would go to him and point out how the people he was trying to emulate were being controlled by the demonic realm. Sometimes they listened, but more often than not, they lived for their flesh and paid the consequences later. They would usually return after they had gotten into trouble and tell me how they wished they had listened to me. I keep praying for them.

There is also sin involving the misuse of sex. God created sex and gave it to us to enjoy, but tells us in His Holy Word that it is to be reserved for a marriage relationship between a man and a woman. Any kind of sexual activity or sexual relationship outside of that is sin. The world would like to redefine marriage and other boundaries for sex, but it's not up to us to define. Almighty God, the Creator, set the standard at the beginning of time. The enemies of God would like for people to be deceived, but God wants the best for our lives; He wants us to know the truth. God wants all of us to be with Him in heaven in eternity – but our sins block the way. Most guys (especially) don't understand this.

Heading up the front steps of Hillcrest, I was so jazzed because this year was panning out exactly how I had planned. Having been home schooled most of my life, I had promised my parents that I would graduate from a public school before heading to seminary. Yes, seminary. With a ministerial degree, I could be a missionary anywhere in the world. I would not marry until age 35 and only then if God led me to the right person. But I was in no hurry. Yes, I was working the Plan.

Unbeknownst to almost all except Principal O'Reilly (who had been selected by one of my dad's OCL [Office of Christian Leaders] teams), I was already a certified paramedic, had been trained in all self defense and survival skills (including various methods of killing) by the elite Eagle Team, a covert military black ops group that required yearly advanced training to remain on the Team. As such, I could be co-opted to help swat teams, police, rescue, etc. I was a licensed pilot and also held an undercover position with the local police force at the School. Consequently, I was prohibited from playing any contact sports, but I did work as Coach Davis's assistant. My main job in the School was to try to sniff out the troublemakers – whether they were students or teachers. Therefore, there was a standing "rule" that if I needed to cut class for any reason, it was granted. I was also required to take pre-law classes in order to word my reports with the appropriate legalese. None of the teachers or school staff knew – just Principal O'Reilly. He was a good Christian man and consulted me often with student issues. I considered him as more of a friend than a superior.

As I walked through the double front doors, I was almost immediately thronged by a sea of students – girls continually flirting, the guys talking sports and wanting to know what I was doing to stay in shape – nothing about learning – just fluff stuff. I still loved it. I was a popular, good-looking, strong guy with an unapologetic Christian perspective on everything. Everyone knew I was a sold-out Christian, not a Christian who played church, but one who quoted scripture, tried to help everyone in need and counseled those willing. And they still wanted to be around me. Go figure!

This was the standard until around the end of October. Then SHE showed up. I watched her enter the same doors I had just come through. Only later did I realize that I wasn't the only one watching her. There wasn't anything that stood out about her, but she had my attention as soon as I saw her – just a mousy looking girl whom everyone was calling one of those "cult" Christians. She wore the same outfit every day – white buttoned-up blouse, long blue denim skirt, black ballet flats. No jewelry – not even a cross. She carried a worn, but clean, canvass bag that she used to carry books. I noticed, also, that she kept a perpetual smile on her face. But I thought to myself "She may dress like a Christian, but all similarities probably end there."

She was walking down the hall with the guys jeering at her and the mean girls laughing at her. Head down, she smiled at everyone and just passed through them, seemingly oblivious to their remarks. I watched her. She glanced at me and held the look for a micro-second. This time, I was immediately struck at how beautiful she was – a natural beauty, not one achieved with makeup. She had brownish-blonde hair that fell in curls down her back, and very tan skin. Well, I thought, she can't be too prudish if she's lying in the sun. But I felt sorry for her. It wasn't her fault she was too brainwashed to get out of a cult. Confident in my ability to categorized people, I came to an instant conclusion about her – probably Jehovah's Witness or Mormon, low self esteem, average IQ, low bar on her future – main goal was marriage, have 2.5 kids, etc. I wasn't often wrong about those things. With her exit, I turned back to the surface conversations.

When I got to Public Speaking Class, she was already there, sitting in a desk they had added to the back of the row next to the windows. What was she doing in this class? It was normally reserved for the best students. My desk was right next to hers and I knew she would be another girl who would develop a crush on me. Every day I cleaned my locker of cards and notes that were slipped in through the vent openings. Ever since the day a very risqué picture fell out of one of the cards, my mother did not want me to look at them or read them. I just gathered them and handed them over to her. I didn't care. Well, I would deal with her crush when the time came. I made a point to ignore her at all costs so she would get the message that I was not interested. After class, I realized she had not even looked up from her notes, let alone look at me. Good! But somehow that realization unsettled me.

Later, I saw Bryan halfway down the hall, waving for me to join him for lunch. I always made a morning stop at Chick-fil-A and bought enough lunch for three or four people. Since I had secretly arranged for Bryan to get an unlimited access lunch card, sometimes he went through the line and sometimes he ate what I bought. My dad saw to it that their rent was paid as well. He had never known his father and I was glad to offer any brotherly advice – especially advice from the Word of God. I had led him to Christ early last year and he seemed to have a hunger for more – even in the midst of the highly-sexualized high school culture. He could see through the game and was very adept at rebuking spirits and covering himself with the Blood of Jesus Christ. Any leftover food went to Bull, the homeless veteran who lived in the park. Bull always met me with a smile and filled me in on the park news of the others who stayed in the shadows. My Dad had already put a word to the Police Chief not to harass him – unless he became a nuisance, which he never did. Bryan loved photography and making videos, so I had given him my old Nikon D70 camera and lens, along with my old Sony video camera with all the attachments and bags. I had also given him my "old" laptop that just happened to have the latest video editing software. He had become the de facto photographer and videographer for the School – chronicling the various events from the year for the web site and print media.

Bryan had an uncanny ability to spot the students who were dealing with issues with parents, teachers, or just simple peer pressure. He sought out those and ministered to them in many ways and they opened up to him. Everyone liked Bryan and friends always flocked around him like they did me. He was also very careful with the girls. He did not want to lead them on. He believed, like I did, that God would lead him to the right one.

I saw her as we walked into the lunchroom – her back to us, sitting by herself, looking down as she ate. She was making periodic notes in a hard-bound, gold notebook – similar to the personal journal I always carried in my backpack. What an odd creature – cute to look at, but odd. When Bryan walked by, he said, "Hi Kristi." She looked up at him, smiled and went back to her book, not even looking my way. I was immediately struck at how much more beautiful she was when she smiled, which she seemed to do easily. Something strange went through me, how pretty she was, but I dismissed it as Bryan and I prayed a blessing over our lunch. We tore into lunch as Bryan and I talked and laughed. When the bell rang, we gathered our trash and I noticed she had already quietly left. The table was clean and her chair was pushed back to the table as it was found. No sign at all that she had even been there. Somewhere in my psyche, an approval mark was registered.

2 HALLOWEEN

Kristi's Journal – October 28: I don't really want to be here, but I keep reminding myself that this time next year, I will be back in Africa. I really missed my friends and the people who had become my extended family. I think my parents missed it too, but the area we had lived in had become too dangerous. They didn't have any friends here and daddy had to take a job at Value Mart to make ends meet. We all felt really alone. We witnessed to sinners, but we didn't socialize with them. *And have no fellowship with the unfruitful works of darkness.*

We rented a small, two-bedroom, one-bath house and daddy had a garden. Momma and I kept the house clean, but because we came with so little, it was sparse. Discovering we were fresh off the mission field, the landlord (a Christian with a heart for missions and missionaries) had arranged with his church to provide the furniture and kitchen supplies we needed because we arrived here with virtually nothing. None of the furniture matched, but that was of little importance to us. Momma seemed happy to have her own little house to take care of. He also delivered toiletries and cleaning products every month or so from the food bank at his church. Daddy would never accept food, though – knowing how God had always provided. In addition, the previous renter must have left their little dog because she kept hanging around our back door. She was so dirty and hungry – just a little fluffy black dog whom we named Molly. We bathed her and my mom treated her like a baby. But she followed me around well, like a little puppy. We adored this little dog.

I was glad this little dog came into our lives because I was their only child and they knew I was going back to Africa as soon as I graduated (or as soon as I could raise the money to go back). They seemed to change the subject when I started telling them my plans. I hadn't made many friends here and hadn't really met anyone that shared my interests. They seemed to all judge me because of the way I dressed. Why were clothes such a gauge of success here? I just kept praying that their eyes and hearts would be open to God's truth. JESUS was the only way to the Father, and He always looked at a person's heart and not the designer wraps.

There was one Christian boy who went out of his way to befriend me – Bryan Roberts. He loved Jesus and invited me to their Bible study on Friday afternoons after school. I couldn't attend because I had to catch the bus home. I also met Richie who wants to be a missionary and we talk often about his plans.

I had never experienced being bullied before, but I did have my fair share of dealing with demons in Africa. That's all this was too. My heart went out to Sasha especially. I knew that she had so much pain from somewhere to have such a need to hurt others. For some reason, she wanted me to KNOW that she and David were dating and she went out of her way to reveal very personal details of their dates. I got the message loud and clear that I was to stay away from him. That wouldn't be a problem. I had no desire for any kind of relationship. If she ever truly accepted Jesus, she would be such a powerful woman for God – just like Paul had been after the Damascus Road experience. My goal, though, was to get through this year as quickly as possible and JESUS would see me through this. *Thank You, Lord, for providing all our needs. You're a good Father and only does good. Hallelujah!*

* * * * * * *

I didn't see her again for several days. Heading to my locker, I saw the beautiful and popular Sasha Ferguson with her copy-cat best friends Felicia and Roxanne in tow. They were leaning over Kristi, at her locker, whispering something. As I passed, I heard something about a sale at Thrifty Mart and it was clear Sasha was making fun of the way she dressed or something. I ignored them (pick your fights carefully) and opening my locker, I gathered the notes and cards, and stuffed them into my bag to give to Mom later.

I was very close to my parents and I told my Mom everything that was going on in my life. Even though I was already 18 (would be 19 in November) she and Dad both gave me incredible freedom. Mom had always warned me about not getting too full of pride and to always keep it in check. There was a very real danger of being influenced by girls with the Jezebel spirit, resulting in life-altering trouble if I succumbed to their charms (literally and figuratively). Most guys never realized that when they had sex outside of marriage, they took on that person's demons and vice versa. The Bible was very clear about those sins.

Even though I worked out almost every day, I wore oversized shirts so no one could really tell anything about my physique or strength. I didn't want to flaunt it, but needed to be ripped for the times throughout the year when I trained with the incredibly tough, covert military Eagle Team. I also did not want to elicit lust in women or men. Mom kept warning me to keep my pride in check which a lot of body builders had problems doing.

Seeing me, Sasha ran over to talk to me about some nonsense, smiling sweetly and closing in a little too much into my personal space. Dressed in a very short skirt; I'm sure she thought it was the height of fashion. In fact most girls dressed that way. The only guys they were attracting dressed like that were the guys who wanted a different kind of friendship. I broke away as quickly as possible. She knew I didn't like her, but that didn't stop her from giving me notes and cards – all reeking of perfume – which were never read, just tossed. Her family was very rich and she dressed in the finest this small town had to offer. Even so, to me she still looked like a hooker. But the way she constantly bragged about what she had and belittled others who had less was a major turn-off. She drove a BMW convertible and was the envy of every girl. She seemed to always be surrounded by jocks and her groupies who took their cues from her by bullying others. All the jocks wanted to date her, but she seemed to put all of her energy into pursuing me. Fruitless endeavor! Sadly, I knew what her life would look like in ten years. One or two divorces under her belt and still searching for something to fill the void that only Jesus Christ could fill. *"God, please open her eyes to Your Truth."* However, I knew that if I tried to convert her, she would feign salvation as just another way to get near me. Ask me how I know.

I was pleased that her comments did not seem to bother Kristi at all because I saw her smiling at a few people as she walked down the hall. But then I was bothered that what Kristi was feeling was even a concern to me. I kept watching her. She stopped to talk to Richie who was a fine Christian young man. He would be perfect for her. As soon as I thought that, I felt a twinge of something. What was this? I needed to get a grip! She was so pretty though when she smiled. Smiling easily is always a sign of emotional stability. I kept watching as she disappeared around the corner

* * * * * * *

As I entered Speech class, I saw her ready for class to begin – head in notebook, hair curling around her shoulders. I almost reached out and touched her hair, but I caught myself. What is wrong with me? I sat down and glanced at her. No response. In fact, she seemed to burrow down even further into her studies – knowing full well that I was looking at her. Mr. Watkins gave the assignment of our next speech to cover our goals for post graduation and we were to start an outline in this class. That would be an easy assignment for me, so I pulled out my laptop and started typing. I noticed Mr. Watkins stopped by Kristi's desk to hover over her. She kept working, so he ambled off to another desk.

Mr. Watkins tended to become a bully at times, but I had already logged some episodes I was keeping an eye on. He seemed, however, to be on his best behavior when I was in his class, but I had heard things he had done in his other classes. I wouldn't do anything unless it got worse and I could document something specifically.

When I glanced at Kristi, she was writing in her gold notebook. I was pretty sure it wasn't about the assignment. Why was I so concerned about her? I was just captivated by her. These were very new feelings for me. Must get more disciplined. Listen, David, stay laser focused on the 5-10 year plan and don't let ANYTHING get in your way – especially cute little mousy JW girls! You've got too much to lose if you get caught up in juvenile dramas. There was nothing that could get me off course. I wanted to do everything I could to serve Jesus. I had never dated, had never even kissed a girl and didn't want to start anytime soon. My goals were the most important aspect of my life, aside from living for Jesus and being chaste while doing it!

* * * * * * *

One day after school, I was standing next to my Hummer (which I had nicknamed "Samson") to see if Bryan needed a ride. I always got to school early, so I was able to get the better parking space in the shade. There she was – walking to one of the school buses on the very end. She smiled sweetly to a few people, but didn't go out of her way to start conversations. She must be very shy. Most people with low self esteem were shy and probably why she ignored me. Bryan bounded up to Samson, but said he was going to watch ball practice with Jonny. Out of the blue, I said, "Bryan, how do you know that Kristi girl?" "Oh, that," he said. "I dropped some books one day and she helped me pick them up, so we started talking. She and her parents are from Africa and just moved here. You should get to know her. You two have a lot in common." Africa. Now my curiosity was really piqued. That would explain her tanned skin. Why did I care? She wasn't my type – too mousy and insecure, but she was pretty and there was a quiet elegance about her. Just something I couldn't categorize. Oh well. I didn't need to get involved with that; I had too many goals to accomplish. Hallelujah!

When I walked in the house, Mom and our housekeeper, Helga, were talking in the kitchen. I hugged mom and threw the cards on the table, along with my journal. I didn't keep anything from my Mom. I loved her so much. She and my Dad were my staunchest supporters and I shared everything with them. They were as excited about what my future would hold as I was. Plus, I really respected them both. They were strong in the Lord and loved helping others. I wanted to be just like them. I knew I would make them proud as a preacher, but, oddly enough, they never pursued that subject with me – even though I talked about it a lot.

Helga and Norbert lived in the house at the front of our estate. In fact you had to drive through their driveway to get to the gate of our house. We had designed that configuration on purpose. To the casual observer, it was an elegant white house backed by a mass expanse of acres and acres of woods (my Grandfather's legacy). Both Helga and Norbert helped with our various missions and knew more than anyone about us and how we operated. Both had been through intel training and knew the importance of keeping secrets. Originally from Bavaria, they sometimes resorted to feigning language limitations when confronted with overly inquisitive people. Mom and Helga (who was like a member of the family) loved to read the silly cards and my journal.

I made notes of things that happened throughout the day and they loved reading about them in my journal!

* * * * * * *

I was watching her walking down the hall when she dropped some papers. She crouched down to pick them up, and Zach chose that moment to knock her further to the floor. She landed on her knees and dropped her book bag. Zach just kicked it further away and was about to push her again, but he saw me and ran off down the hall. I picked up her book bag while she was gathering the papers, not even looking up. I held out my hand to help her up. As she put her hand in mine, she looked up at me. Suddenly I gasped as an electric shock ran through my body. She slowly rose with her hand still in mine just looking at me. I said nothing. Primarily because I was in shock. She gently said, "My books." Still, I couldn't speak as I held out the bag. She pulled back her hand and took the bag. As she walked away, she said, "Thank you, David." I was still standing in the hall as a statue. A mute statue. I couldn't believe what had just happened. Suddenly, I wanted to talk to my dad. He would know what this is. He would also know how to fix it . . . if that's what I wanted. At the moment, I didn't want this fixed. It felt so right. *God bless you, Kristi.*

* * * * * * *

The next morning when dad and I were working out, I asked him about what happened. He just said, "I don't know, son, but the same thing happened to me with your mother. My advice is just ask God to lead you." Great advice, but I felt this was much deeper than what dad had experienced. But I decided to back off from her and get back to my plan, and, of course, God had other plans.

Today was "spirit day" at school to celebrate the demonic Halloween. Of course I didn't celebrate anything that had so much of the devil in it. If people only knew the demons they were attracting when they listened to certain music, watched certain programs or movies, and especially what they chose to do on Halloween. The demonic realm was very real, but most people never associated sickness, poverty, and addictions to generational or open-door curses. Most people were dressed in costumes of the most garish nature. God help them. Bryan, Stephan and I decided to have a prayer meeting while everyone else went to the Gym for the Halloween Festival.

I saw Kristi sitting on the edge of the big concrete steps leading up to the school. She was talking to a girl dressed as a fairy. Kristi was holding her hands and the girl had her head bowed. She was witnessing to this girl. Wow! While everyone else was serving satan, Kristi was leading someone to Jesus and being the apostle Jesus told us all to be. Then I remembered if she was a JW, she would *not* be leading someone to Christ. I hoped that girl didn't start going to Kristi's JW church. Talk about the blind leading the blind. Another positive mark registered, though, and I was still having those strange feelings about her. I needed dad to give me more information about these things. I needed details!

Somehow the Halloween masks and costumes brought out the devil in people. Some were so made up you didn't even know their identity. I was just inside the door when I noticed Dracula blocking Kristi's entry. She moved to one side, but he blocked her. She tried several times again, but he kept blocking so she turned around to go in another door. He bounded down in front of her and roughly grabbed her arm. What was he trying to do? She was trying to pull away from him, but he was too strong. I knew he was hurting her. Something went through me; I couldn't explain it. I ran down the stairs and gripped the same arm he was gripping her arm with. I pressed in as hard as I could. I am very strong and I know he got the message.

"Hey, Drac. Can't you see she doesn't want to play your game?"

He dropped Kristi's arm and bolted. She was rubbing her arm and my heart was hurting for her. I wanted to put my arm around her, but that would be too forward. She looked up and said, "Thank you. He didn't hurt me really. I'm tougher than I look." She looked up at me and laughed. I know I looked at her like "Are you for real?" Most girls would have played the victim card to get my attention.

She said, "It's not that bad, really, but thank you. You are a good person – you take care of so many people." Why would she say that? She didn't even know me. In fact, wouldn't even look at me. But I said, remembering the fairy girl, "And so do you." She smiled at me the way she had smiled at Bryan that day. My heart was racing and singing for joy. I thought, "David, get a grip." But somehow I didn't want to get a grip. I was beginning to really like her and want to know more about her. Plus, she exuded such a positive energy which I knew was a spiritual force. There was no way she could be in a cult with that spirit. She was the embodiment of the scripture: *A soft answer turneth away wrath: but grievous words stir up anger.* Was she that wise I wondered?

Bryan was waiting for me as usual before our next class began and he had seen me looking at Kristi. He said, "Why don't you ask her out?"

"Ask who out?"

"Kristi."

"Bryan, don't be ridiculous. That's ALL I need is another girl making goo-goo eyes at me all day and leaving notes in my locker. No thank you!"

"Kristi's not like that. She loves Jesus and follows His Word. She's not a fake Christian."

"How do you know?"

"Because I know her. She is very particular and won't go out with just anyone because they ask her. She's sweet and has very high standards. In fact, I know several who are planning to ask her out. But you should ask her. I dare you!"

"Bryan, I'm not interested in dating anyone. I have way too much on my plate right now, plus I'm not about to trifle with some young girl's feelings just to prove a point to you."

"Okay, David, your loss," and walked away.

We would look ridiculous together anyway. I was very neat about my appearance and she was too, except her clothes were a little too casual and, well . . . plain, for my taste. And kind of mousy – but I had always liked mice. But what Bryan said kept nagging me.

Bryan knew what he had seen. David was attracted to Kristi, he just didn't want to admit it. He knew David and now he knew

Kristi – they were perfect for each other, but he seemed to be the only one with this revelation. Let's see what I can do to facilitate this union. He knew, though, he couldn't use conventional tactics with David. He was patient and knew a plan would come to him.

* * * * * * *

Later at lunch, Bryan noticed that Kristi was only drinking water. Was she fasting? He didn't know, but if it was something else, that could be remedied. He met David at his locker.

"Hey David. Can you give me a couple of chicken sandwiches for lunch? I'm planning to have lunch with someone today and I want to bring the lunch – and when I say I – I mean you. You bring the lunch."

David laughed and threw two CFA bags at him. "You weirdo." And David walked down the hall.

Bryan saw Kristi making notes in her journal and drinking her water. He stopped by Kristi's table and said, "Hey, can I join you?"

She said "Of course!"

He threw a bag at her and said, "I was supposed to have lunch with someone else, but he bailed, so you can have this if you like."

Kristi looked at the bag. She was so hungry. Her mother had forgotten to give her money for lunch this whole week. For supper they were having Raman noodles and they were all quiet around the dinner table. It just wasn't enough. She seemed to stay continually hungry. But Kristi said, "Oh, no, Bryan, give that to someone who's hungry."

He said, "Well, if you don't want it I'm just going to toss it."

Quickly, she said, "Don't do that; I'll eat it."

She had already noticed how much perfectly good food was being thrown into the trash. So many people could have used that food – especially her!

They both ate lunch and talked and laughed. The more Bryan was around her, the more convinced he was that she was perfect for David.

Bryan decided he would not divulge the particulars of this lunch to David. He was still trying to formulate a plan to get them together and didn't want him to pity Kristi. He needed to recognize that she was on his level in every way.

3 NOVEMBER

A new guy started about a week after Kristi arrived. His name was Chance Russell and talked incessantly about his being a youth leader in his church, how good he was at *any* sport, and generally talked about himself a lot. The rumor mill was abuzz about him getting a girl pregnant at his last school, but those were just rumors and I wouldn't repeat them until proved otherwise. But to the unsuspecting, he looked like an upstanding guy. He was good looking and really built, so the girls were flocking around him. I caught him staring at Kristi several times, but she didn't notice him at all – like she didn't really notice me. I hoped she would see through his façade and not fall for him like the others.

One day I saw him at her locker, with his big muscled arm possessively grasping the top of her locker – using the cat method of trying to appear larger than they actually were. There was an instant reaction in my gut. What did I care? Maybe I wanted to look after her like I would my sister or something. She was just such an easy target for the school bullies and I wished she would just hit them back with their own tactics. But she never would – just kept quiet until they tired. I couldn't understand my reaction to the situation, but I did linger at my locker to keep an eye on the her. Kristi was nice enough around him, but from what I could tell, did not give him any indications that she wanted it to go further. When I saw him walking her to her next class, I was very unsettled. He seemed so forward with her. Why didn't she stop him? I did notice that she did not look up and smile at him like the other girls did when they were around him. In fact, she seemed annoyed by his continued presence, but I imagined she was too shy to protest his advances. I was forced to follow them to my class and when she was about to turn into her room, he put his arm around her. She broke away quickly and darted into class. Was that my answer? However, it was none of my business and I was going to stay out of it, although I did keep thinking about the situation throughout the rest of the day.

I watched them both. I saw him talking to other girls, but whenever Kristi was in the vicinity, he made a bee-line to her in order to hover over her and perform cat-expansion. After a few days of this, Kristi quit going to her locker. I supposed she got her books early and lugged them around all day just to avoid the creep. By now, though, he knew her class schedule, so he rearranged his "run-ins" with her accordingly. Of course, I was following all of this – and not covertly either. I'm pretty sure he knew I was tailing him. He was now being so forward with her and putting his arm around her anytime she was around. For some reason, this annoyed me greatly, but I didn't want to get involved, although that didn't stop me from following them both. But I couldn't get involved anyway unless I saw him hurting her. She would have to get the courage to deal with the matter. "God, please help her."

My God. In Him will I trust.

* * * * * * *

The bell rang for the entire school to congregate in the assembly hall for announcements, so everyone was rushing and I was running late and bringing up the rear. From my vantage point further down the hall, the crowd was heading, en masse, down the big staircase. When I reached the stairs, most everyone was gone, and I almost considered running the stairs two or three at a time to catch up, but something slowed me down and compelled me to look back at the top of the stairs. That's when I saw Sasha sneak up behind Kristi as she was headed down. Sasha pushed Kristi – hard! Kristi lost her balance and was headed to crash headlong down 20 steps. I lunged sideways and caught her in mid air. She was clearly frightened and held on to me tightly. We were so close I could feel her heart racing. I'm not sure, but I think I pulled her closer. She did not protest. Instead, she looked in my eyes and said, "I'm so sorry; I must have tripped." WHAT? Kristi was taking the blame for what Sasha had done.

Incensed that she had taken the blame, I said, "You didn't trip – Sasha PUSHED you." Sheepishly she said, "Well, I'm sure she didn't mean to." I couldn't believe she was making excuses for that bully. It could have been a serious injury. A little angry that she was covering for a bully, I said, perhaps a little too sternly, "Well, the next time you're going down stairs, look around and make sure no one is behind you. And take the less traveled side of the stairs." Looking at me with those beautiful eyes, she nodded and sweetly whispered "yes."

I was still holding her close, but now, clearly uncomfortable being so close, she pushed away. Her arms were surprisingly strong and I could tell that the strength did not end there.

Straightening her clothes, she said "Thank you for helping me . . . again," and continued down the stairs, this time holding onto the handrail.

Had she sensed my thoughts? A light floral scent lingered and I hoped that it would stay with me throughout the day.

When I got to the Assembly Hall, I pulled out my journal and logged the episode. I was feeling that strange feeling again. I looked around for her but didn't see her. I think she was behind me because I could almost "feel" her. So many odd feelings. "Lord, what is this? Do you want me to help this girl somehow? Please show me Your Will. Thank You, JESUS!" I had long ago learned to ask the Lord any question. He was faithful and just to answer and guide me. Yes, I walked a very supernatural walk with Jesus and I wanted His answer and approval for anything I was dealing with – including a new friend. I wondered if Kristi had a relationship with Jesus like I did. Not many people did, I knew. If people only knew how much Jesus wanted their fellowship. He wanted someone He could talk to. Hallelujah!

Okay, I admit I was still following her. I just liked being around her. Maybe Bryan was right about asking her out. That way I could get to know her better, but then I would have to deal with the consequences when she fell way short of any expectation I had, even though, on the surface, she exceeded *all* my expectations. If that changed, however, then I would have to carry the guilt of her broken heart.

I just couldn't understand all these new feelings. I saw her head into the Library for study hall, so I decided to skip class and spend the hour studying also. I gave her a few minutes to settle in. I went to the bathroom, made sure I looked okay and went into the Library so it wouldn't look like I was following her – which I was. She wasn't there. Had she left when I was in the bathroom? "Lord, please show me where she is." Then I remembered some small tables in the far back behind some seldom used reference books and out-of-date subject books – my secret hiding place. Somehow I knew that's where she was. I made my way around the corner to the secluded space, and she looked up at me as I entered.

"Oh, hi hon – Kristi." (I had almost called her "honey." – bullet dodged.) Moving toward the table, I said, "I come back here a lot. It's a lot quieter."

She moved to get up. "Am I in your seat?"

"Oh, no. I'll just sit over here," and sat at the table next to her, facing her. The tables were so close we could almost touch each other. I was still in awe that she was ready to give up her seat for me. Now who would do something like that? It just spoke volumes of her character. I wanted to be able to look at her, but I was happy just being near her. I wanted to ask her so many questions, but I made it a point to not look at her at all for at least 20 minutes and pretend to study. I started making notes and "studying." After a while, I stretched out my legs (the tables just didn't accommodate my size) and I looked over at Kristi. She was looking down at my stretched-out legs. What was she thinking? I looked away so she wouldn't catch me staring at her. I prayed, "Lord, please help me with this. I do so want to know her better, but she's so shy."

* * * * * * *

Kristi's Journal:

Why does my heart beat so when he's near me? I know Sasha suspects I encourage him, but he seems to always be there when the bullies find me. I found myself looking at his legs. They looked so strong. It reminded me of Samuel, who was so strong and muscular. David reminds me so much of Samuel who was so strong and kind. I imagined David lifting weights. I should leave. My thoughts are not pure. "God, please forgive me." Why is he always around me when I'm trying to avoid him? I'm not his type. He needs someone on his same social status – but not Sasha. She wasn't right for him. I need to study and not study him!

* * * * * * *

After reading a while, I got a little tired, so I put my head down on my books away from Kristi. Sweet sleep must have overtaken me because after a while, I felt someone gently shaking me awake. I turned and there was Kristi, kneeling down to me at eye level – and oh so close. But she had to be because the tables were so close. Still half asleep, I moved in to kiss her, but she backed away. She lost her balance and grabbed my thigh and at the same time I reached out to grab her arm. We were holding each other like this and just looking at each other. What was she thinking? But the way she was looking at me – did she want me like I wanted her? I knew this was against my "plan," but I really did want to know her better. No, I wanted to *hold* her in my arms.

She looked down at her hand on my thigh and jerked it back. Then she stammered, "David, the bell rang and you need to get to class."

Not fully awake, I nodded. What had just happened? She turned and ran out. I couldn't follow her because I had to get my books together and go to class. I couldn't afford to miss too many classes. I wasn't that special.

In the next class, I furiously logged every detail in my journal. I could still feel her hand on my thigh. If I could just process this, I could understand it better. I then remembered my prayer and realized Jesus HAD helped me when I had prayed. I never dreamed that the entire episode would end with my being so close to her and almost kissing her – something that felt so right. "Thank You JESUS!"

A few days later, I saw her again in Speech Class. Head in book, she didn't even look up when I sat down. That annoyed me in a way I didn't understand. In fact, she never looked my way during the whole class, but I did see her pull out her journal and start writing. She had just flipped to another tab when Mr. Watkins said, “Kristi, did you hear the question?” He must have used such a low voice, I hadn’t even heard the question. She said, “No, Mr. Watkins, but if you can repeat it, I’m sure I can answer it.” I knew it was happening. He would use this situation to start “bullying” a timid, guileless girl and my defenses were on high alert.

“Kristi,” he continued “I am not in the habit of having to repeat my questions. Now can you answer or not?”

He wasn’t even giving her a chance and I knew she would be intimidated by him. Every muscle in my body was tense. What would I do? I had to act wisely.

Looking directly at him, she said calmly, “Mr. Watkins, I apologize for not giving you my full intention, but I know you to be a fair man and I know that you care more about our learning than you do about scoring innocuous ‘points’ that have nothing to do with our studies. So if you could repeat the question, I’m sure I could answer it.”

By this time Mr. Watkins was turning red with anger. She had just eviscerated him in front of everyone, but only the most astute could surmise the meaning of her words.

“So, you don’t know the answer?”

“Mr. Watkins. I don’t know the question and I have apologized for not paying attention. Most good teachers would *want* their students to be able to answer questions they’ve been taught. Most teachers also know the difference between making a point – in this case the importance of paying attention – and damaging someone’s esteem by trying to intimidate them in front of everyone. So if you could repeat the question.”

Everyone gasped – including me. I could not believe her ability to stand in the face of such a trial, yet she let students bully her every day. I used this opportunity to stare at her – because everyone else was also. It didn’t faze her. She just stared at him.

Now redder than ever, Mr. Watkins said, “Okay, Kristi. The question is: what was the impetus of Churchill giving his radio address to the nation?”

Oh no. I didn’t even know that answer. I didn’t even remember reading about it. There was total silence in the class with everyone’s attention on Kristi and Mr. Watkins.

Kristi, looking straight at him, said: “Well, that scenario doesn’t appear until Chapter 10 and we won’t cover that chapter until next week, but the answer is because he had boarded a train in London’s new underground railroad and talked to several average citizens about Germany, Hitler and the possibility of war. Their answers provided him with the information he needed for his address to the Nation.”

Everyone was shocked that she apparently had already read ahead to that chapter and at the same time outed Mr. Watkins for his unfair teaching tactics. Then everyone (except me) turned to watch Mr. Watkins to see how this would manifest. He was standing there, looking at Kristi with such anger. He was absolutely twitching with unrestrained excitement thinking of ways to further demean her, but he certainly didn’t possess her diplomatic demeanor. Just then, the bell rang and seemingly saved her from further abuse – but I knew this wasn’t over by a long shot and he was the one in control.

I stood up and waited for her. I wanted to warn her about Mr. Watkins’ retaliatory tactics. Well, really, I just wanted to talk to her and be near her. I had to know more about this unique girl.

She gathered her books, and her precious journal (was my name in that journal?), and started to walk out. I joined her when she came out. As we walked down the hall, I said, “Kristi, please be careful with Mr. Watkins. Sometimes he does not use maturity when dealing with students. In fact, he can be a regular Hitler.”

She said, "Well, we should pray for him to find another vocation. Some people should not be teachers. But I only have a few more months of school and then I'll be gone. I can handle him."

As she turned down the hall for her next class, she turned and said, "Thank you, David, for your concern."

Her words struck me to the core. She, the true Christian, wanted to PRAY for him, while I wanted to retaliate. However, I logged this episode in his ever-growing file. If he tried any sort of retaliation against Kristi, I would finally have the evidence I needed to do something about him.

* * * * * * *

Kristi's Journal:

I had a very bad day in Speech class. So much so that I don't even want to record it here. Mr. Watkins has never really liked me. I have seen how he looks me up and down and I know he doesn't approve of the way I dress and he sneers. Yes, sneers. After today, I'm sure he will do everything he can to fail me. I just have to keep my grades up to prevent that. He just hates me and can't hide it. He keeps giving me dirty looks. I try not to look at him at all. But it was wrong for me to do what I did. I shouldn't have questioned his authority. Lord, please forgive me. And I will ask Mr. Watkins for his forgiveness.

I would write a note to Mr. Watkins apologizing for my challenging his authority. I feel I was in the right, but he was the one with the power to flunk me, so I shouldn't be so dogged about being "right." Just a few more months in this horrible school and then I would be free. *Thank You Jesus!*

* * * * * * *

A few days later, heading to my locker, I heard some guys laughing and "posturing." I knew the sound and knew someone was being bullied. Three of the biggest troublemakers – Zach, Larry and Dean (I had already started a file on all three) – were standing over something against the wall. Kristi! She had her head down, back against the wall with her book bag over her chest. She didn't look scared, just trying to be patient until they grew tired of the game. Had she learned this technique in Africa?

I walked right up to the group, held out my hand and said, "Kristi, are you ready to go?" She looked up into my eyes, as if trying to read my meaning. As she grabbed my hand, the three quickly dispersed down the hall. I suspected one of those guys still had bruises from our last encounter. She held my hand tightly and I was glad. I was feeling the same electrical charges I felt the last time she held my hand. When we turned the corner to go into the main hallway, she quickly dropped my hand, mumbled a "thank you" and went over to her locker. The crowd was staring at us.

I walked to my locker and took out the books I needed. My head was spinning. She wanted nothing to do with me. What was this? I could have my pick of girls. Oh no. There was that pride Mom was always warning me about, but it was true. The girls were so forward and bold. They let me know that they were willing. It was a complete turnoff for me, though.

"Father, please forgive me for that pride. I am nothing without You. Please create in me clean hands and a pure heart. Keep me humble to do Your Will."

I felt that peace come over me and I knew He had forgiven me. Everything would be okay. I just had to sort out all these new emotions I was experiencing. She was definitely different. I knew, though, if I pursued a friendship with her (in order to get to know her better), it would lead to a broken heart for her. She would start to like me and I just wasn't into that – I couldn't be. I had to follow my plan and relationships weren't part of that. But she was sweet and I was very impressed with her Christian maturity. She could teach me a few things – like forgiveness and praying for others.

Bryan had witnessed this entire event and he was pleased. David didn't come to just anyone's defense, but David always hated to see anyone bullied. He would just have to wait to make his move, which was okay because he was patient and he had the whole school year to go. He saw Richie come around the corner. Richie was also a solid Christian and very good looking. Girls flocked around him too, but he was oblivious to the attention. He stopped and said something to Kristi and Kristi laughed. Unbeknownst to many, Bryan knew Richie had a girlfriend who was already doing mission work in India and Richie planned to join her after graduation. A plan was forming within Bryan's brain, but he would have to work this carefully. He KNEW David and Kristi should be together. "God, please help me get these two stubborn boneheads together."

4 NOVEMBER: WEEK 3

I was in the locker room one day when Chance was changing out. He was bragging to some guys about a bet they all had. I overheard only portions. “She's a virgin . . . probably never been kissed . . .Those types are easy . . . I'll have her before the end of year.”

My chest tightened and fury flooded through me, but I was able to keep it in check. The thought of him touching her enraged me. He was about my size, but no match really. I knew he was talking about Kristi. I had to warn her, but we hardly ever spoke now – just exchanged some looks that further served to confuse me. Primarily because of the electric shock that went through me every time I looked into her eyes. I really did want to know what she was thinking. She clearly, though, had NOT developed the crush on me like the others. I was disappointed at that, but glad at the same time. If she were too easily available, I probably would have lost respect for her. Would she be wise enough to resist

Chance though? I was going to add that situation to my prayer list. Lord, please open her eyes to what's really going on with Chance.

Since I got to school early anyway, I decided to stake out her early morning locker runs and tell her. She had to know. She may want nothing to do with me, but something in me wanted to protect her and I still imagined her in my arms.

The next morning I was there bright and early and I didn't have to wait long. She rounded the corner and, seeing me, she abruptly stopped and just looked at me.

"Kristi, I have to tell you something."

She inched closer and my heart beat faster, "What is it?"

"That guy Chance. I don't think he has your best interest in mind."

She lowered her head and said, "I know, David, I don't know what to do about him. He won't leave me alone."

My heart jumped for joy. She had not been fooled by him. And I loved the way she said my name. "Do you want me to have a talk with him?"

"No, I will handle this on my own. I'm tired of carrying a whole day's books around just to avoid him."

"Okay, just let me know if I can help."

She looked up at me with the most beautiful eyes I'd ever seen. The more I knew of her spirit, the more beautiful she became to me. My heart was pounding just looking at her. Everything about her looked so soft. I could NOT be feeling this way – I loved it and I hated it. I had no control when I was around her. She flashed that beautiful smile and said, "David, you are so kind and I appreciate it, but I will be okay. I've put up with much worse than anything Chance could do. Thank you for being such a good friend."

She turned back to her locker, got her books and walked to class. I expected her to look back at me and smile, and I waited with anticipation, but she walked on. Why was my heart beating so fast? I was standing there just stunned. What just happened? She had all but dismissed me, but did it in a way that was so gracious and kind. And called me that "F" word – *friend*. Suddenly, I had a vision. She was in my arms and we were lying together, so different from when I just imagined it. This seemed so natural and not in a sexual way. But I still wasn't sure – was it a vision or lust?

Okay, this was ridiculous. I was going to get a grip on my emotions and would NOT be led down this road – whatever road it was. I had a solid future planned for the next ten years and it did not include a relationship – unless the Lord led me. But He was the One who had given me my five- and ten-year plans. Confusion reigned, but I knew who the author of confusion was. Maybe the evil one had put her in my path to thwart the plans I had for the Kingdom. "Jesus, please help me with these temptations."

Whatever Kristi had said to the guy worked, because the next day he was working on another unsuspecting girl and Kristi was free to come and go as before. Truthfully, I was disappointed because I had come to like being her personal rescuer. Who was I fooling? I just wanted to be near her. I heard in my spirit: "Look around you." It was then I began to notice that other guys were doing the same thing I was doing – studying and looking at her when they thought no one was looking. Guys who hung around Sasha were only doing so because they thought she was loose, but it was different with Kristi. They respected her and I could tell most were already in love with her. Well, I didn't have time for that but I would look out for her – just to make sure no one tried to hurt her. After that I really did try to avoid her, but I liked looking at her all the same. Even so, I couldn't seem to erase her from my mind. My thoughts continually replayed every moment we had been together. Then it happened.

I was watching for her (yes, I admit it), but she didn't come to her locker as usual. Was she avoiding me? What an egotistical thought (again). "God, please show me if she's feeling what I'm feeling. If she doesn't care, Lord, can You show me?"

I kept waiting to catch a glimpse of her, but the last bell rang, so I would be late and my class was two floors down. I started to run down the now-empty stairwell. Not expecting to run into anyone, I charged right into someone coming up the stairs. I hit them so hard, they almost fell backward down the stairs, so I grabbed her waist. It was Kristi. I couldn't believe I was holding her again, but this time, we were holding each other. She was holding on to my shirt sleeve. We were so close, our bodies crushed together. In an almost imperceptible movement, we moved closer – almost as if we had missed each other the days we hadn't seen each other and we wanted to be together. We were just looking into each other's eyes. Time stood still. All I could do was whisper her name – "Kristi." I know – or maybe hoped – that she was feeling what I was feeling. But maybe she was holding me so tightly so she wouldn't fall backwards. I couldn't think of anything else to do but send more subliminal messages. "Don't you see what is happening here? Can't you see we're meant to be together?" Then she slowly made her way around me, still holding onto my shirt and looking into my eyes. Then she broke away and ran up the stairs. I just stood there hoping she would come back. Then I remembered that she HAD moved in closer. Was that my answer? That she really did have similar feelings or was it because she didn't want to fall?

After that episode, she flooded my every thought. I didn't know if I wanted her out of my mind or not. "God, will You please show me Your Will in this?" I didn't like the term, but she truly had bewitched me. "God help me." This wasn't like God to abandon me when I needed Him and I needed to HEAR from Him. "Please show me, Lord."

I then went to Principal O'Reilly's office to explain how Kristi was being bullied, so she had begun getting her books when everyone had cleared out. This made her habitually late to classes, but she wouldn't file any complaints against fellow students. I asked him to alert her teachers to excuse any time she came in late for class and to not count any lateness as demerits against her grade. He agreed and also wiped out any that were already on her records. I think he already knew some of the situation because as I was leaving, he put his arm around my shoulders and said, "Thank you, David, for looking out for these students." I smiled back at him and said, "Thank you for doing the same."

* * * * * * *

Kristi's Journal:

I ran into him again (literally). I was trying to get to the Library but had avoided going to my locker until the last minute so I *wouldn't* see him. I just couldn't be having these feelings for him. Sasha sees everything and has ramped up her abuse. There were just days when I didn't have the strength for the unending comments from her and her group. I was going up the stairs to my locker when someone coming down hit me hard. I almost fell backwards. But he caught me. And held me. We were so close. I tried to grab his arm, but his arm is so big and I only had one free hand, so I just grabbed his sleeve. He held me so tightly and so close. We just stared at each other. It happened so fast, I didn't have time to get nervous. In fact, I liked having him hold me. I felt no guilt from these feelings. But soon I came to my senses. It would be a wonderful fantasy if David was not defiled and he was as nice as he seemed, but that wasn't likely. And God had promised me an undefiled man. I made my way around him. I couldn't stop looking at him, but I broke away and ran back up the stairs, forgetting to thank him.

I must stay on my course and not let anything get me distracted. The thought of him and Sasha together, kissing, just made me hurt inside for some reason. Maybe I just wanted something better for him. She wasn't right for him, but neither was I. He would just have to work that out on his own. *Father, please help him.*

* * * * * * *

I was selected to give my speech first. I loved this stuff. I had given many speeches throughout my life and I loved the response from people. They seemed to hang on every word. I talked about my five- and ten-year plan after graduation; helping my parents with several state-wide missions; and the plan for seminary after working with my father's missions for a year. Then my plan was to pastor a church.

The talk lasted about 30 minutes, then we closed with a Q&A session. Of course Sasha raised her hand with the first question. I pointed to her. She stood and asked, "I didn't hear you say anything about marriage or a family. What are your plans for those?" I said, "Those are very personal decisions between God and me; I will follow His direction."

Stephan asked about my workout schedule and I told him every morning at 5:30 my dad and I worked out for an hour. I answered several other questions, then I saw Kristi raise her hand and I pointed to her. She asked quietly, "Please tell us your experience of how the Lord called you to preach." I could see she was really curious, but suddenly, I was nervous – yes, NERVOUS. Why?

I said, "Well, I've always wanted to be a preacher since I was a young boy. Whenever anyone asked me what I wanted to be when I grew up, I said 'a preacher,' and I'm pretty sure that's what God wants me to do."

She said, "Yes, but most men that God has called know exactly what transpired when they were called to preach. It's a very real, divine experience."

I couldn't believe this. She was trying to trip me up. After all I had done for her, she was deliberately trying to sabotage me in front of the class. Now who was the bully? No she wasn't a bully – I knew that. I was so confused. Not answering, I just stared at her. She stared back. What was she thinking? Fortunately the bell rang. I grabbed my books, gave her an angry look and stormed out of the classroom. I hope she got the message that I did not appreciate her sabotaging me like that and in front of the whole class. Only bullies did things like that. I had certainly misjudged her!

I had a math test in the next class and I finished early, so I started writing in my journal about the previous class episode. I wrote out every detail about the sabotage. Was she learning Sasha's bad habits? When school let out, I dashed to my locker, packed the notes and headed out. I was still so perturbed and hurt about what she had done. I tried to think logically. Maybe, just maybe she was merely innocently asking a question. Or maybe she wasn't the sweet little innocent girl I thought she was. Then I remembered that JWs put a lot of stock in religious nonsense. But I just couldn't stop remembering how beautiful she looked every time our eyes met. What was happening to me? I would get her out of my system if it was the last thing I did!

When I got home, I threw the notes and journal on the counter and ran upstairs to change. I just wanted to go run for an hour to clear my head. When I got back in, Mom was standing at the kitchen island where everyone seemed to congregate. Handing me a neatly folded piece of notebook paper, she said, "You may want to read this one." I unfolded and read the neat, compact handwriting:

"David, please forgive me for asking that question in class. I did not mean to cause you frustration; I just thought it would help so many to hear your testimony. *We overcome evil by the Blood of the Lamb and the word of our testimony.* You have been so good to me and I truly do value your friendship. I am sorry if I spoke out of turn or if I said anything to embarrass you in any way.

You are such an incredible Christian leader in this school and so many look up to you. I would never want to do anything to damage that. I admire your strength and compassion when dealing with others. God bless you in anything you decide to do. Your friend, Kristi."

My heart was racing; my mind was spinning. Who IS this girl? This was so beautifully written – not the writing of an insecure person or saboteur at all. Was I wrong about her? *God, please help me.*

Mom looked at me, sensing my dilemma. "Who is Kristi?"

I said, "She just moved here from Africa."

"What was she doing in Africa?"

"I don't know."

"I read your journal. She didn't mean anything with her question. Don't hold that against her. In fact, she's right. Your dad and I think you should be really sure about what God wants you to do, and pastoring a church may not be it." She knew being a pastor would be so limiting with all of David's God-given talents.

"Mom, what are you saying – that I shouldn't go to seminary?"

"I'm just saying to be sure about what God wants you to do. Your options are much more vast than the average person. You have so many talents, David – far above the average person AND pastor – that being a pastor may not be God's Will for you. Just ask Him what HIS WILL is. That is the greatest gift you can give yourself." She knew her son. He wouldn't be happy with the limitations of being a pastor. But she would have to let him come to that realization himself.

"What's her last name again?"

"Day. Kristi Day. She started here around the end of October. That's all I know about her." I didn't want mom to know my dilemma with her and all of these new emotions.

"Day?" I wonder if her parents were missionaries. John and Ally Day were the reason your father and I got married. They spoke at our church about their mission in Africa and when we heard them speak, we both knew we wanted to be missionaries.

Ask her tomorrow if you get a chance."

"Sure Mom."

* * * * * * *

That night I had a dream. I was walking down this road alone. The trees and flowers felt "happy" as I walked. A gentle breeze blew my hair and it was the perfect temperature. The flowers released a medley of fragrances and I was so happy. I had smelled that floral scent somewhere before. Then I felt someone walk up behind me. I turned to discover it was Jesus. I dropped to my knees and bowed before Him. He reached out His hand to me which I eagerly took. As I held His hand, an even greater happiness and pure joy spread through me. We walked for several minutes, not speaking because we knew each other's thoughts. When we passed by a group of tall, flowering rose bushes, someone walked out of the bushes and joined us. Jesus held their hand. I kept trying to peer around Jesus, but when I did, He seemed to grow bigger and smiled at me because He knew I was trying to see who else was walking with us, but He wanted to keep it a secret from me. We came to the end of the lane to a big, flat rock. He held my hand as I stepped up on the rock, then let go. When I turned around to face Him, I woke up. I knew this dream was significant.

What was He trying to tell me? "Jesus, please reveal to me Your message. Thank You for caring about me. I love You!" I could smell the flowers all around me and I remembered the floral scent around Kristi. Then I remembered Kristi looking at me in class. Her eyes were searching mine with true compassion – what I had interpreted as sabotage. Why was she so beautiful? What was happening to me? "*God, please help me!*" I fell back to sleep thinking of her. This was hitting me hard!

* * * * * * *

Kristi was to give her speech next. She walked up to the podium and stood quietly, head down. I felt sorry for her and wished I could elevate her self esteem. Some people (Sasha, et al.) started to snicker. Then I saw her whisper "amen," and realized she had been praying. She straightened, looked directly at the class and began: "My parents were missionaries first in a remote village near Malawi, formerly a British colony known as Nyasland, where I was born. We lived in the village and I grew up with many brothers and sisters. In small villages, we all look after each other – especially in Christian villages. When my parents first arrived, the entire village worshiped demons. The witches and shamans put curses on my parents, but they rebuked the evil spirits and covered themselves with the Blood of Jesus and were therefore protected. One night the witch doctor told the entire village that my parents would be dead by morning. The villagers waited all night, heard no screams and burst into my parents' hut the next morning to see the damage. Mom and dad were already having breakfast and when they saw the villagers, my father said, "Our Spirit is much greater than the tiny spirits you serve. Would you like to have the Spirit that is with us in you?" The entire village was converted. When the witchdoctor saw that my parents were still alive and all the villagers had left him, he let out a scream and ran into the jungle. He lurked around the outskirts of the village for several weeks and my father went to him and told him about Jesus. He was converted and my father cast the demons out of him. For several days, there was a real struggle for his soul, but Jesus won! The villagers had called him by a name of one of the demons, but after he was saved, he wanted everyone to call him "Jantu," which was the name his mother had given him.

My father said that when he and momma arrived, the village was dirty, the children were dirty, the huts and grounds were littered with trash and bones. There was little food and it seemed the entire village was generally sick. Several women were barren and many villagers had died premature deaths. There was also an old gnarled tree in the middle of the common area that was twisted and dark and never seemed to produce new leaves. This was the tree they dedicated to their idols and chanted and danced around. Within months of the conversion, the villagers started cleaning their children, their huts and their grounds. My father gave them seeds that he had blessed and dedicated to the Lord. The seeds grew in their gardens; the gentle rains watered them and the sickness disappeared. Everyone walked around with joy, thanking Jesus continually. One night during a thunder storm, lightning hit the tree and it burned to the ground. When that happened, my father said that you could feel the remaining evil spirits leaving.

While the men were hunting or working, the women would have to walk several miles for water, so my father wrote a letter to the home church in the U.S. Within weeks, a mission crew from the church came and dug a well. They also built an outdoor pavilion for church services. Before long, it was standing room only in the outdoor church where my father, mother and others would preach. My father would lay hands on the sick and they would be healed; he would cast out demons and pray for people for anything that was needed. He prayed for barren women to have children and God blessed them. He trained many preachers from that village who later converted other villages. Momma would pray for the women and teach them about God's love. God was really blessing their ministries. These people had first-hand knowledge of how the devil would steal, kill and destroy, but after accepting Jesus, they all began to walk in the favor of God. We rarely had to depend on a miracle from God, but even then He didn't disappoint. Hallelujah!

Since I was born in that village, the villagers treated me like I was one of their own. I learned to hunt and fish with the young village children and catch things to eat. We learned to walk quietly to sneak up on our prey. We set traps and caught our food. There were several times other tribes would try to steal from us, but each time they were caught. Because of all our prayers, we knew that angels were guarding our village. We did not have them arrested or punished. We told them about Jesus and many accepted Him. Many former criminals are now preachers all over Africa.

Eventually, however, the guerillas discovered our paradise and began their rampage against sweet, loving Christians. They hunted us and brutally killed anyone who would not convert to their religion. They hated us. But they hated Jesus and He did nothing to harm anyone. He said in His Word, "they hated Me and they will hate you also," so we were expecting the attacks. We kept moving from place to place, but finally my parents deemed it too dangerous to stay, so we moved here. I made them a promise that I would graduate from high school before I became a missionary also, which is my ultimate goal after graduation."

The room had been totally quiet while she spoke, and were devouring her every word. Then she said, "So, that's my story. Do you have any questions?"

Every hand was raised. Some didn't even wait. "Did you ever see or kill a lion?"

"Well, I have seen many lions and I'm sorry to say that I have killed one. They're such majestic creatures, but while hunting one day, I saw one about to charge a little boy whom I dearly loved. I was very accomplished with a bow and arrow and I brought it down in one shot. Most villagers used spears, but another missionary had given me his bow and arrows and taught me how to shoot. I know I had some angelic help because I had asked God to help me before I shot."

"Did you have a boyfriend in Africa?"

"No, I've never had a boyfriend, but there was a warrior that all the young girls had a crush on – me included. He was strong and fearless and was a true man of God. He was known throughout the entire region for his bravery, and he was respected by his friends and enemies alike. The guerillas had a standing order to have him killed on sight, but he escaped capture every time. God was truly protecting him and his team. He had a team that he had trained in the art of warfare and together they would attack the guerillas while they slept. They would take care of the guards, steal their food and weapons, and then give the food to the poorer villagers. He never divulged what he did with the weapons. His name was Samuel. His parents and grandparents were Christians who were converted at a Reinhard Bonnke crusade. When Samuel was born, he was dedicated to the Lord – just like Samuel in the Bible. He was one of the bravest and strongest men I've ever met."

When she said that, my heart was pierced with jealousy. I could see she still had feelings for this man. While I "played" at being a warrior, he really was one and twice the man I was. I've never been jealous in my life, but I was jealous of this man who had Kristi's heart. My head had been reeling throughout her entire speech. What I had mistaken for meekness was an incredible strength and fortitude like none I had ever seen – including my own!

Sasha piped up: "Why do you wear the same clothes?"

The entire class seemed to be angry and embarrassed for Kristi at her question and gave Sasha disapproving looks.

Kristi smiled patiently as if having to speak plainly to a child. "Most village women don't really care about how many dresses they have; they're mainly concerned with the character of a person. They usually have about two or three dresses and don't have a spirit of covetness on them. If another woman or child needed clothes, the women would donate from their own sparse collection and somehow the Lord would always repay their kindness. These women know that loving each other is much more important than what someone is wearing. Their values are very different from here in the U.S. These are the values these women taught me and I hope they carry me through life."

"What church do you go to?" someone asked.

"Well, we don't really attend church, per se; we just follow Jesus and try to be like Him in everything we do. We have 'church' every day in our home. We read the Bible, we pray, we have devotion and we bless each other. It's one of the best ways to start any day."

She started to say something else, but then just said, "Thank you for letting me share with you today."

The entire class was silent and you really could hear a pin drop. Kristi gathered her notes and started to walk back to her desk. The entire class (except Sasha) stood up and started applauding. This clearly embarrassed Kristi and as she sat down, the bell rang. Students thronged her. I wanted to be among them, but my heart and mind were racing. Mr. Watkins was the one who really hated that her speech had been so well received. He was fuming. I could almost see his thought processes and I knew he was devising another plan to retaliate against Kristi.

I had to go process all of what I was feeling and what I had just learned. My next class was study hall, so I went to the Library, pulled out my journal and wrote and wrote. Boy, had I been off the mark with my initial assessment about her. I had been wrong on every one of my points. *"God forgive me for judging her."* She wasn't a JW or SDA or Mormon or Catholic. She didn't follow any man – just Jesus. Thank You JESUS! I just knew I wanted to know more about her. Her self esteem was MORE than okay. Praise GOD!

Still thinking of her, I walked into the lunchroom looking for Bryan. I stopped cold. Richie was sitting with her. They were talking and laughing. I sat down at a table behind them. They seemed to really like each other. Unlike Chance and Zach, Richie was an upstanding, strong Christian. I didn't know him well, but I knew he wanted to be a missionary. Would he be the one to go with her to Africa? My heart was beating so fast. What was this? I was worried and anxious. Richie had moved in while I was trying to sort out my little egotistical feelings. How could I have thought I was the only contender? And I could tell she *liked* him. Maybe I wasn't ready for her, but I didn't want anyone else to have her. *"God, please help me."* My heart stopped when I saw her reach across the table and put her hand on his hand. I couldn't stand it any longer. I wasn't hungry anymore; my stomach was in knots. I got up and left.

If David had bothered to look around, he would have seen Bryan two tables away. Bryan had been the one to suggest to Richie that he ask Kristi about being a missionary. He also suggested Richie buy her lunch for the valuable information she could provide. He had also witnessed everything that had just transpired with David. David had come into the lunchroom at just the right time. He had seen David sit down and not take his eyes off of Kristi (and Richie). And Kristi patted Richie's hand at just the right moment. David finally got up and left without even having lunch. Yes, this plan was coming together better than expected.

* * * * * * *

Kristi's Journal:

I talked to Richie today and he wanted to have lunch with me so he could ask me questions about being a missionary. He is such a sold-out-for-Jesus Christian and he loves helping others! He insisted on buying my lunch because he said it was a fact-finding mission, which worked out for me because momma had forgotten to give me lunch money. He is so funny too, which will come in handy as a missionary. It's a lot harder than people could imagine. He told me of his girlfriend already in India and he couldn't wait to see her and join her on the mission. I will add them to my prayers.

5 MR. WATKINS

After that, I looked for her everywhere I went. She must have sensed this because it became increasingly hard to spot her. Was she hiding? She couldn't have been hiding from me because she didn't even know I was looking for her. She must be getting all her books in the morning and returning them in the afternoon to avoid any encounters. I was certain she didn't know I was one of the stalkers, I mean lurkers. Turning down the main hall, I saw her standing with Bryan, Katie and Jason. Richie was nowhere in sight. Hallelujah! She was laughing and talking in an animated way I had never seen. She was so pretty, and laughed so easily. I ducked around the corner where I could just watch her without having to worry about others accosting me.

I just kept looking at her as she was laughing. She was still smiling when she looked up and saw me. The smile immediately disappeared and we stood staring at each other. About that time Sasha possessively grabbed my arm and pulled me to her. An anger hit me – a *righteous* anger – and I decided to stop this girl once and for all. I leaned into her, smiling, and said, "Get out of my face and stay the hell away from me!" She immediately dropped her arm from mine and darted around the corner. I looked up at Kristi who had witnessed the entire thing. A crestfallen look came over her and she darted down the stairwell. Oh no, she probably looked at me smiling at Sasha and thought I had said something intimate to her. I ran after her, but she was nowhere in sight. In a way I was pleased that she may have been jealous, but I wanted her to know the truth regardless.

For the next several days, she was all I thought about. No doubt about it, I was already in love with her. I just wanted to be with her and decided to throw caution to the wind and ask her out. I was so nervous, but I knew if I planned out everything, it would make it easier for me. I would wait until after school and look for her as she was heading to her bus.

I saw her again as she walked down the hall. I just couldn't stop looking at her. Bryan ran up to her and she stopped to talk to him. They both laughed and I was struck at how beautiful she looked when she laughed. Something happened in the core of my being when I saw her laugh. Bryan handed her a note and she walked on. What was up with that?

I walked up to Bryan, "What did you give to Kristi?"

"Oh, nothing really."

"Come on, Bryan. You know I need to know these things."

"What do you care? You said yourself she wasn't your type."

"Well, I do care about her and I've seen some guys trying to take advantage of her, that's all."

Bryan was really enjoying this and his plan was coming into play.

"Look, David. Just forget about her. People, and by people I mean GUYS, are really warming up to her. I think she's moved on, if you know what I mean."

David's countenance fell. "Moved on? What are you talking about?" I knew he meant Richie, but why didn't I see them together?

"Just forget about it. Got to get to class. See ya later buddy," and took off down the hall.

Was she interested in someone else? Who else had moved in? Is that why she had been MIA? Why didn't I see her with anyone? It was always with a group – not just one guy.

David made up his mind, he would ask Kristi out before it was too late. He just wanted to get to know her better and he couldn't get a handle on all these new feelings. He just felt right around her. *"God, please help me."*

I was waiting by Samson, waiting for her to go to the bus. When I spotted her, I ran to her and said, "Kristi, I would like to talk to you if you have a minute."

"Well, I don't really. I have to catch my bus."

"I can take you home."

She remembered Sasha said that she and David had been going together for almost two years and she certainly didn't need any more trouble with Sasha. "No, I don't think that's a good idea. I need to catch my bus. See you tomorrow." And off she ran.

* * * * * * *

Kristi's Journal

I can't be having these feelings. He's not right for me. I know he's been with Sasha or is dating Sasha, but if that's the case, he certainly doesn't treat her well. Every time I see him he's surrounded by pretty girls. He must be dating them too. Why did my heart beat so when I was around him? On the surface, he has the veneer of perfection, but what secret sins was he hiding? Someone that good looking could not also be honorable with all the pretty girls flocking around him. *"God, please help me with this. I need Your strength to help me through this."* But I have decided to avoid him at all cost.

For some reason, the teachers have stopped admonishing me for being late to class. I would rather be embarrassed in front of the class instead of being abused at my locker. However this happened, I know God is in control. *Thank You JESUS!*

* * * * * * *

I came home with a heavy heart. I didn't even want to hide it, but I didn't want to let mom know how vulnerable I was feeling. I wanted to tell her everything, but I just couldn't right now. I had never felt so low, but I just had to regroup and devise another plan. But for now, I just wanted to be by myself and lick my wounds. Today I did not give her my journal – just the cards. I had too many notes about Kristi that, for some reason, seemed too personal for mom to read. I changed clothes and ran to the lake house I had built last year about a mile from the main house. I planned to move there at some point, but I would let God tell me when. I went into the craftsman-style bungalow which needed to be swept and dusted. It had kitchen appliances and supplies, a sofa, dining table and bed, but that was it. One day my desire to furnish it would return.

I laid on the bed and thought about every time I had an encounter with Kristi. Then I fell asleep. When I woke, I remembered the dream with her taking center stage. I wanted to be with her, but she had been in love with Samuel – who was a real warrior – respected by friends and enemies alike. I only dreamed about defending the innocent; he really was. I was so jealous. And now other guys were trying to date her. This did not make me feel better. I went back to the main house just in time for dinner. I ate a little something and tried to make conversation. Mom sensed something wasn't right and tried to keep the conversation light and uplifting. She knew I was feeling down. But she couldn't help me with this.

I went to my prayer closet, knelt down and started crying to God. *"God, I know You've put her in my life for a reason. Lord, I love her – is she the one You are leading me to? Lord, I need You to show her. Thank You, LORD, for leading me and guiding me."* A peace came over me and I went straight to bed.

* * * * * * *

It didn't take long for Mr. Watkins to show his vindictive nature. Almost at the end of class on Friday, Mr. Watkins instructed us to read the next chapter. While the rest of us turned to the next chapter, Kristi pulled out her journal and started writing. Mr. Watkins must have been waiting for this very moment, in fact had probably orchestrated this "study session" to act on his plan.

He walked up to Kristi's desk and grabbed her journal. He said, "Well, let's see what she's writing that is soooo much more important than this class, shall we?"

Kristi was in shock and clearly upset and kept trying to grab her journal as he swatted her hand away from the book.

He started reading: "Seeing Africa will be such a welcome relief. I just miss my family there so much . . ."

Intense anger filled every fiber of my being. I jumped up and grabbed her journal from him. He had no right to be doing this and I would make sure he didn't. I towered over him and looked at him with defiance. "Mr. Watkins, you've gone too far this time."

He glowered at me and said, "David, give me that book and YOU (sticking his bony finger into my chest) report to the Principal AT ONCE!"

I didn't move, but I still had possession of her precious journal. Glaring back at him, I was all but daring him to hit me. About that time the bell rang, but no one moved. Everyone wanted to see how this would play out.

I went to my desk, gathered my books and held out my hand to Kristi. She eagerly took my hand and followed me out the door. I really didn't know what to say to her. In fact, I didn't say anything at all. I just gave her the journal, looked into those beautiful eyes, and walked to Principal O'Reilly's office. I was pleased, however, that she just stood there watching me walk down the hall.

* * * * * * *

The next time I went to Speech class, we had a new teacher.

I looked over at Kristi who was absorbed in her book. She still would not look at me. "God, please help me." A storm was brewing outside and it looked like it might get pretty bad. We had already been assigned to read the next chapter in our book, so our new teacher, Miss Jenkins, could get up to speed on where Mr. Watkins left off. Even though the class was quiet, there was a strange energy in the room – almost electric.

Kristi kept looking nervously out the window and I could tell she was very afraid of storms. What precipitated that fear? It must have been something that happened in Africa. With each clap of thunder, she jumped. Suddenly a loud clap of thunder sounded just overhead and a bolt of lightning lit up the darkened sky. The other girls screamed, but Kristi sat frozen, looking out the window. Miss Jenkins instructed the people sitting next to the windows to move their desks away from the windows and share desks with the next row. I was ecstatic – Kristi and I would share.

Kristi just sat there not moving – just looking out at the storm. I reached down, grabbed the metal rung at the bottom of her desk and gently pulled her over to my desk. I slid my book away and moved her book in the middle so we could both share. Kristi had not moved during all this and was still looking out the window, so frightened. I put my arm around the back of her desk so she could have more room to "study." Another clap of thunder with lightning almost immediately following and she backed into my chest completely. Her hair was touching my face. It smelled like flowers. I was touching her shoulder and I could feel her trembling. I wanted to just hold her and tell her everything would be okay, but I didn't want her to bolt.

I leaned in and whispered, "Kristi, the Lord did not give us a spirit of fear, but of power and love and a sound mind. Jesus continually told His disciples 'Fear not.' Remember, He held up His hand to the storm and said 'Peace, be still.' His words are for us today. Fear not Kristi."

Those words seemed to break the spell she was under. She slowly moved around almost facing me. She was so close. And I just stared deeply into her eyes. I knew people were staring at us but I didn't care. I knew she wanted to draw closer, to put her head on my shoulder. Could I really tell what she was thinking now? No, but I could read her spirit. I could have nudged my arm to draw her closer, but I didn't dare do that either. We were both bound by our mutual respect for each other. Plus, I knew the teacher might not like it and want to separate us. I just looked at her trying to send her a subliminal message: "Can't you see how I feel? Can't you see how I care for you?" She must have felt others staring because she looked past me and whatever she saw changed the atmosphere between us. She didn't look around. She just turned to her book and pretended to read – anything but face me with the earlier closeness. I knew she was pretending because she never turned another page just kept staring down at the book.

Eventually the storm moved on and everything returned to normal. Well, not quite. I was no longer the normal person I was when I walked into that class. I didn't care. She was the most precious thing to me – except my love for Jesus. I knew she was the one God had chosen for me.

When the bell rang, I walked out with her, taking her hand. I needed an answer. She did not pull away from me. I turned to face her.

"Kristi, are you seeing Richie? Are you seeing anyone?"

She looked up at me and said, "No, I . . .I'm not.

We were still holding hands. Suddenly, she pulled her hand from me and made a bee-line to the ladies room to get away from me I was sure. I supposed I had made her very uncomfortable being such a bulldog in this circumstance. But I had my answer. *"Thank You JESUS!"*

* * * * * * *

Kristi's Journal:

A thunderstorm hit in the classroom today and it took me back to the time in Africa when Keyason and I were sitting together in the outdoor church. We were both about 8 years old. He was the youngest of four boys and three sisters and we were great friends. We were singing and playing and laughing, when suddenly lightning came out of nowhere. I was knocked ten feet away and when I came to, a few people were by my side, but most were huddled around something on the ground. It was Keyason. He had been killed. One minute he had been singing to Jesus and the next minute he was with Him. I was so very sad though.

Every time a storm came through after that, I always hid under tables and beds and whatever was handy. There was nowhere to run today. I was in the middle of class. The new teacher had given an assignment to read. I couldn't just run out of class and hide in the bathroom – which is what I really wanted to do.

David came to the rescue (again). I don't remember how or when, or why really, but he had pulled my desk next to his during the storm. I tried to be strong, but I was so scared. David was so gentle and caring. He quoted scripture to me and spoke softly to me about the power of Jesus. That was exactly what I needed to hear. The Word is so powerful. *Thank You Lord!*

I know he likes me, he held me so close – too close really, but I wanted to be in his arms. I felt so safe. I just wanted to put my head on his shoulder. As I was leaving, he grabbed my hand and we walked out together. I looked up in time to see Sasha giving me a dirty look. I knew immediately that her abuse would take a darker turn because of this. I know I should ask him to leave me alone. He is not right for me. I wish he were undefiled and liked only me – but that was a fantasy not likely to happen. But I could dream about it. In fact, I did dream about it.

I will deal with Sasha like I always do: ignore her and keep praying for her. Maybe I should just tell David to leave me alone. His attentions were causing me too much trouble with her.

I could write him a note, thanking him for his Christian concern and quoting scripture (that really calmed me), but that I would really appreciate it if he would stop looking at me and following me. I can't imagine why he's doing this. We're from two different worlds. Why are these temptations hitting me so suddenly? I'm not experienced in these things like most Americans are. I know I'm too naïve to even think about any type of relationship. I would be too easily fooled and I had a mission to run – in AFRICA! And far away from the evil entity America had become. Daddy told me when he was growing up, there was scripture reading and prayer in schools and very little rebellion and violence. People had respect for each other and each other's property. What happened to the Country that was also responsible for the world hearing the Gospel?

I will just write a note to David thanking him and when I have the opportunity, I will talk to him face to face. IF I could talk to him face to face. I was always so nervous around him for some reason.

He always looked so handsome and dressed so well and always had the perfect response for any situation and, for the first time in my life, I felt "less than." I never felt that way around anyone. What did he see in me except another conquest? I just didn't want to be a number in a long line of girls. *"God, please show me what I should do in this situation."*

6 THE WITCHES

Jesus told us that whatever we bind on earth shall be bound in heaven and whatever we loose on earth will be loosed in heaven. Consequently, every time I walked into school, I could feel the evil spirits that operated in that school. Most students (or adults for that matter) did not know how many doors they willingly opened for the demons to attack them. If they could only see into the spiritual realm for three seconds, every one of them would be on their knees asking Jesus to save them. Each day before I entered the doors, I bound and rebuked evil spirits and covered myself with the Blood of Jesus.

Somehow, the school witches knew I was doing this, but they couldn't touch me with their spells. They knew firsthand that the Holy Spirit in me was much more powerful than the weak counterfeit spirits in them. How sad that these people would be so fooled into thinking their demons had any kind of power over true Christians. How could they serve created beings when they, themselves, had been created in the image of God with the BREATH of God breathed into them, and, therefore, anyone who had accepted Jesus had far more power than the little created beings they thought had power.

They always congregated at one end of the hall so they could analyze the students to determine which ones they would recruit for their coven and which ones they would cast spells on. You could easily spot them – not only because of their black, demonic attire, makeup and tattoos, but from the red string bracelet with the seven knots they all wore on their left hand. It was like a calling card. If only the general populace knew. People who embrace darkness never get what they want – or expect. In fact, they dig themselves deeper and further away from the One who created them and could easily save them from this evil.

So many are unaware of the witchcraft all around us -- especially in the mainstream churches. Satan knows that as a created being, his words are powerless. He needs a human body to SPEAK those words or spells, or *any* words of death really, so he tricks them into thinking he has so much power and that they are subject to him. Jesus said, "My words are spirit and they are LIFE!" God's Words spoke the world into existence, so, since we're created in His Image, then our words have far more power than any demon. They trick so many people because we are not taught how to put on the full armor of God and rebuke evil thoughts; to fight even on a basic level. If only they knew that JESUS is the Way, the Truth and the LIFE and NO MAN comes to the Father, except by Him. *THANK YOU JESUS!*

The leader was a girl named Rhonda, but she had changed her name to Lilith (the name of a demon) in Junior year. I still called her Rhonda openly and almost dared her to pull something. I had hoped that her inability to affect me would not go unnoticed to the girls she had recruited, but they all seemed to be, well, spellbound. They tried to copy her in everything – including putting curses on Christians who were unfamiliar with what the Word said about the demonic realm.

She kept trying to put curses on me, but I knew the Word. A curse without a cause could not light. Plus, she was so ignorant of the Word of God, if she sent a curse, it would return to her seven fold and, according to her witchcraft "rules," it might come back to her TEN FOLD. She couldn't understand why accidents and weird things kept happening to HER immediately after trying to put a curse on ME! I knew, though, that if I won her to Jesus, she would be a most powerful leader in the Kingdom of God. I would keep praying for her. God knew His plan for her life and maybe he would use me to help her. I would just keep an open mind about it. He said in His Word, *"Do good and bless those who spitefully use you."* I would do everything in my power to do that, but I would also fight this evil.

They were congregating again around lunch break. They rarely ate anything, just stood in the corner and did their chants. I spotted Katy, a sweet, unsuspecting sophomore who had no clue who they were and they were calling to her. Oh no. She didn't know what she was walking into. I said a quick prayer around her and covered her with the Blood of Jesus. I decided to warn her later.

While I was standing there watching them, I noticed Kristi walking down the hall. I couldn't help it, I had to keep looking at her. She was so beautiful. When I looked back at the witches, Rhonda/Lilith was looking back at me. An evil smile formed on the black slash that I supposed was her mouth. For a brief moment, fear tried to rise up because I knew she had caught me looking at Kristi and must have realized how I felt about Kristi. I wasn't worried for myself, but about what she might do to Kristi and her family. I instantly rebuked the spirit of fear and I loosed the spirit of peace and joy over me and Kristi. I then covered us both with the Blood of Jesus. I knew Kristi and her family had dealt with demons in Africa, but she probably had no clue that they were just as prevalent in America.

"Lord, in the name of Jesus, I bind any demonic spirit sent to attack Kristi and her family in any way, I break their power and send them to the feet of Jesus for Him to judge. I send any and all curses directed at me, Kristi or her parents back to the sender. I cover her and her family with the Blood of Jesus and thank You, Father, for protecting them."

Rhonda/Lilith walked past me, but still had that demonic smile on her face. I decided that after I talked with Katy, I would also warn Kristi.

The next day, I sat in my truck and prayed protection around me because of what I knew I had to do. I walked into the school to search out Katy and made my way to the witches. As I turned the corner, I saw Katy in the group and almost didn't recognize her. She was dressed all in black, with black dyed hair and garish black eyeliner and lipstick. She looked just like them. *"God, please help me and protect me with what I'm about to do."*

As I was walking I saw Kristi headed straight for the group. Rhonda saw her and immediately put out the alarm to strengthen their "circle." Kristi smiled at everyone and whispered something to Katy. *"Oh, God. Has Kristi been deceived also?"* It hurt my heart that she wasn't more discerning. I stopped at my locker and determined to stay put until I knew what was going on.

Katy and Kristi walked a few steps away, but Rhonda intercepted them. She grabbed Kristi's arm and started chanting. The rest joined her. As soon as that happened, I shut my locker and walked towards them. As I got closer, I heard Kristi saying, *"Father, please forgive these girls. They have no idea what they've gotten themselves into. Satan has deceived them, Lord, into thinking they can have better lives serving the evil one. Please show them Your glorious power is greater than any demonic entity they're serving. Father, in the Name of Jesus, I bind the spirit of witchcraft, the spirit of Jezebel, any demonic spirit they have given power to and we break their power and cast them to the feet of Jesus for Him to do with them what HE will."*

Wow. She was already taking authority. Why was I always underestimating her? About that time, I joined the group and said, *"Father, Kristi and I touch and agree that from this day forward, these demons will have no power in this school, nor against any person in this school. Father, you said in Your Word, where two or more agree, it shall be done and we thank You, Father, that You watch over Your Word to perform it. We put a hedge of protection around those who innocently took demonic vows. Show them Your truth, Lord. I plead the precious Blood of Jesus over us, Lord, for protection."*

When Rhonda heard me say "Blood," she went absolutely apoplectic, and glared at us both before she stormed off. She KNEW she had no power now. Kristi and I walked Katy to an empty stairwell. It was deserted because the bell had rung for class about five minutes earlier. Kristi and I explained to Katy the danger she was in, but Jesus would protect her if she accepted Him.

"Katy, one day every knee will bow – and that includes ALL witches and demons, and every tongue will confess that Jesus Christ is LORD! Now they will bow before Him as His children or they will bow before Him as the Judge that will cast all demons into the lake of fire. You DO NOT want to follow these evil creatures. They don't care about you; they just don't want Jesus to have you. They NEED a human's body to operate."

She repented for the vow she had taken with the witches and gave her heart to Jesus in that stairwell. We warned her that satan would not want to let her go easily and that she was probably in for a battle. We taught her how to rebuke thoughts and evil spirits and how to cover herself with the Blood of Jesus. We asked her to join us for our Friday afternoon Bible studies. Occasionally, we all went through basic self deliverance. It was impossible to live in this evil world and not be affected by the demonic.

When Katy later appeared in the lunchroom, her makeup was already washed off. Afterwards, she never wore all black again; she never wore the garish makeup and her hair returned to its natural color. Praise God!

Several of Rhonda's followers approached Kristi and me to ask for deliverance and we gladly led them to the Lord and administered deliverance. Then we taught them how to self deliver. "You are having trouble and cannot clearly THINK because of your willingly tuning in to Satan's frequencies. Godly soul ties are formed and are good, but when the ungodly soul ties are formed, people control us by the powers of satan's kingdom and we are not free to go forward with the Lord. To get totally free, pray this: *'In the Name of Jesus, I command the demons out of my mind. I repent, break and renounce all legal holds or legal grounds which demons hold over my life. I renounce all my sins in Jesus' name and ask and receive His forgiveness of my sins. Those known about or not known and all those sins that may have passed through my bloodline. I break ungodly soul ties from family members, past or present friends (all living or dead), doctors, psychologists, psychiatrists, psychics, pastors, teachers, etc. and I forgive them. Father we take authority over satan, every demon, wizard and witch, breaking ungodly soul ties from everyone on the earth. We break Satan's powers and his spiritual blindness in Jesus' name. Hallelujah to the Lamb of God!'"*

Kristi and I were ministering *together*. If felt so right and natural.

* * * * * * *

Kristi's Journal:

I am so overwhelmed with these feelings for David. I know he is NOT right for me and is not the one God had chosen, but being around him is difficult for me all the same. He always seemed to be there when the bullies surrounded me, but he couldn't be with me in the ladies room where the most brutal attacks occurred.

Sasha had seen him looking at me several times and she let me know that they had been together for two years, but she let him "use" other girls because that's the kind of guy he was. She said he was only after one thing and called me vile names because of what she perceived as the truth.

Today I walked into the bathroom and she was in there with Felicia and Roxanne. I turned to leave, but Felicia jumped as if on command and blocked the door. Reecy was also there, but she seemed oblivious to the insults and assault. Sasha proceeded to berate me, call me vile names and make fun of my clothes. She grabbed my arm probably wanting me to fight her, but she only succeeded in tearing my blouse at the shoulder. I knew I could easily sew that back. She laughed when that happened with Felicia and Roxanne joining in. "You should quit buying your clothes at Value Mart. They're so cheaply made."

I just stood there and silently prayed, "*God, please forgive her. Help her see Your truth, Lord.*" Somehow her demons knew what I was doing and she manifested more.

The bell had long since rung for class, but she continued the attack. I knew that if I had said anything, it would have further inflamed her and resulted in more abuse. Finally she got tired of my not responding and stormed out. I picked up the books she had scattered and looked at the damage to my blouse. Then I looked at Reecy and said, "She doesn't mean what she says. I'm sure she has a lot to worry about."

Reecy said, "Why don't you defend yourself when she's bullying you? Don't you know she's just going to keep doing it until YOU do something about it? Report her!"

I said, "Reecy, can't you see how much pain she's in? We don't know what she's been through for her to act that way. There must be a reason she wants to hurt others. And we don't know what she may be currently going through. If she turned to Jesus, she would not have that anger and she would know the peace and love of Jesus living inside her."

Reecy looked at me with such hatred, "What does your GOD know about pain and suffering? He's a JOKE! You and people like you and your God have caused more trouble in the world than you can imagine. I want NOTHING to do with YOU or your GOD." She looked at me with anger and hurt. Then she stormed out.

I then realized she must be going through something. I wanted to talk to her. I followed her to a concrete table outside in the courtyard. Thanks to Sasha, we had both missed much of our class, so at this point it didn't matter if I went to class or not.

I walked up to her and said, "Reecy, I don't know what you're going through, but it's clear you're hurting. Please let me help you."

She glared at me with tears welling up in her eyes. "What the hell do you know about hurt? And how can you help me – you can't even help yourself."

"Reecy, these bullies want me to fight with them and that would ruin my testimony. They need Jesus, but they don't know it. They know that there's something different about those who walk with Jesus. I've seen so many people controlled by demons and they don't even know it. I've seen too many horrific things from people being controlled by those same demons to not recognize it in other people. Please tell me what you're going through. I can show you how you will be able to withstand many things in life, but you can't do it on your own. Jesus is the only answer and He loves you. You are His child and He does not want any of His children to suffer."

She glared again, "Then why does He let . . ." Her words trailed off and I could see she wanted to tell me something. Instead, she grabbed her books and stormed off. I then realized that Reecy had probably stayed in the bathroom for me so that Sasha wouldn't get too out of control since Reecy served as a witness to her abuse. I think she wanted to protect me. I felt even more compassion for her. *"Holy Father, please help Reecy. Please protect her from whatever is tormenting her. In the name of Jesus, I rebuke any demonic spirit attacking her or her family, I bind it and cast it to the feet of Jesus. Jesus, please help her. I plead Your Blood over her and her family. God, please bless her. Thank You for answering my prayer. I love You."*

7 DECEMBER

The following days I kept looking for her. I looked in all the usual places. Where WAS she? Was she purposely avoiding me? Now, how egotistical was that thought? Jesus said to bring every thought captive to His obedience. How could I control those thoughts? They seemed so natural and legitimate.

I had scheduled a study period, so I headed up to the Library to make some notes in my journal. If I wrote out my thoughts and feelings maybe I could understand things better. I stopped abruptly at the entrance. There she was, sitting at a table, with at least four books spread out around her. She was furiously writing, so she had not seen me. I stepped just outside the door so she wouldn't see me. *"Lord, what should I do?"* Then it occurred to me to video her. I set my phone to video and placed it in my shirt pocket. I quietly sat down at the table right in front of her. She didn't even look up. I opened my notebook and took out my pen as if I were taking notes in case she looked up. I just kept staring at her. She was so beautiful. I tried to send subliminal messages: "I love you Kristi. Can't you see that? Why can't you see what you're doing to me? God, please show her." Suddenly, someone dropped a book and broke the silence. She turned to see what happened, but then went back to writing. Still, she had not even looked my way. Then I saw her stop writing. She thought pensively for a moment, pushed that book aside and took her journal out of her bag and started writing. Again, I wondered if my name was in that journal.

Kristi's Journal:

He invaded my thoughts again. It's almost like my spirit can feel his spirit when he's around, but I know he's not here. I checked when I came in. But what is this? I just keep remembering all the times he has helped me. He's so good to me, but his being good to me means that he is not being faithful to Sasha. He's defiled and not right for me, so why am I always thinking about him? We're from two different worlds, but yet I dream about him not being defiled. I imagine him honorable and faithful. I imagine him wanting to be with me because he wants a Christian relationship. But I just know that . . .

* * * * * * *

I was hoping the video was good. The phone was a special model with the most high-end capabilities. I could access the video controls from my laptop, but was careful to keep the window minimized in case someone walked up behind me. These were the phones used by the highest-level military intel. No one (except a select few) even had my number. I just kept looking at her. So beautiful, so quiet, so regal. Suddenly, I had a vision: "I was lifting her from Samson and she was holding onto my arms." Then it was gone. *"Father, what does that mean? What are You trying to tell me?"*

Someone made another noise just to the right of me. I had already zoomed in on her and from my peripheral vision of the laptop, I could tell the video was good. She looked up, then saw me. I was looking straight at her. She gasped when she saw me, but kept staring at me as well. What was she thinking? I just kept staring. Then she did what I was dreading. She went back to looking at her journal, but I could tell she was breathing hard and clearly unnerved by my being there. Did she hate me? I just loved her and I wanted her to know it. I could tell my being there was really bothering her because she was still breathing hard. Should I leave? Suddenly, she gathered her books, not even putting them in her bag, and rushed out.

"God, please help me. I know what You've shown me. Can You please show her?"

I stayed in a blue funk until the bell rang. I had never in my life felt such despair. I shut off the video and started to my next class. But I just couldn't do it. My spirit was crushed.

I cut my next class to process all these conflicting feelings. First I went to the cafeteria, just to sit at a table and process what had just occurred. I looked in and saw too many who would want to sit with me and talk and I didn't want to be around anyone except her. I just couldn't settle down enough to process anything. I almost wanted to cry. I then wandered up to the Science Lab which was usually deserted this time of day. I would occasionally go there to study or read. There was a desk in the corner behind some shelving that looked out onto a small courtyard in the back of the school. I put my books on the desk and started walking in front of the windows, pacing and venting almost and practicing what I would say to her when I saw her again. There was something bothering me, but I couldn't figure out what it was. I had had that dream again and I wasn't getting any answers. What was He trying to tell me? *"God, please don't pull Your Spirit from me. Please give me an answer. Show me what You want me to do, Lord."*

I glanced out the window. There she was, sitting with someone. It was that weird Reecy girl. Reecy looked and dressed like a witch, but I never saw her with the other witches. She certainly looked like one, though. She had jet black hair, tattoos on her neck and face and wore weird, unmatched outfits. A real clown and so angry. She walked around with a continual scowl – almost daring people to speak to her. Most knew better. Except Bryan. He seemed to like Reecy and talked to her often. He was a real enigma. Kristi seemed to like her too and obviously didn't judge her like others did. I was immediately convicted because I had just judged her. *"God forgive me for judging Reecy. I don't know what she's been through to be so angry, but You do, Lord. Show me how I need to pray for her. Please help her. And Lord, will you please show Kristi Your Will for the two of us?"*

Kristi was leaning toward her, trying to get her to understand something. About that time, Reecy slapped Kristi! Kristi did not react at all. Every muscle in me tensed. Should I run down to protect her? Kristi then reached for Reecy's hand and held it. Reecy started crying. Kristi put her arms around her and held her. It was so intimate – not in a dirty way. I didn't know Kristi well, but I DID know she wasn't a lesbian. Reecy cried and cried. Kristi just kept holding her – just like we had been trained for trauma victims. But how did Kristi know about that? At that moment I became aware that I was jealous of Reecy. The bell rang and I knew Kristi had English class, but she kept holding Reecy, rocking her, probably knowing this was much more important than any class. It was such a sweet picture and I felt guilty witnessing the scene.

I had never met anyone like Kristi. She seemed to know so much about people and life, and almost every time I saw her, she was doing something good for someone else, when so many were abusing her. Where did that wisdom originate? Her parents must be just as special as mine and I wanted to know more about all of them – especially one of them. I couldn't cut another class, so I left determined to find out what had just transpired between them. I could get a report from mom on Reecy's situation. Mom could get info most others could not.

Walking away, I realized that God had answered my previous prayer. He was showing me so much more than I anticipated. *"Thank You JESUS!"*

* * * * * * *

Alone in my room, I watched the video over and over and fell more in love with her at each viewing. I wanted her image imprinted in my brain. I sent it to myself in an e-mail so I could watch it on any platform. I put it in a folder named "Agape." Man, I had it bad. I didn't care. She was everything to me and I knew God had led me to her. I was still seeking His answers, but I knew He was leading me to something big.

I went the next two days without seeing her. By now I was really hurting. I mean my heart HURT! Was this normal? I wanted to ask my Mom, but for the first time in my life, I didn't want her to know my weakness towards Kristi. Not yet anyway. What was wrong with me? She was so quiet around people, but showed an inner strength I had never seen. I knew I would see her in my next class. After class I would ask her out to dinner this weekend.

When I sat down, Kristi was turned away from me toward the window. She didn't want anything to do with me. Now my heart really hurt. Had I said or done anything that would prompt this?

Had she been so incensed seeing me in the Library? Mrs. Jenkins wanted us to spend the class reading a speech by Admiral Michael Rogers – a national hero. We were to make notes and turn them in tomorrow. I had already read this speech (because he was a true hero to me and had read most of his speeches and had already pre-ordered his upcoming book), so I just quickly made some obligatory remarks so I could spend the rest of the class trying to get her attention. I kept looking at her, but she was almost completely turned away from me. Then I saw it. Tears were streaming down her face. Someone had done something to her. Had Zach finally gotten to her? I had often heard him bragging about his conquests and that if they didn't deliver, he would "take it." The thought of him even touching her made me want to seriously hurt him. I wanted to hold her. Instead I pulled out my handkerchief, touched her gently on the arm and gave it to her when she turned. She took it, but not looking at me, said "thank you." What was hurting her so much? If I found out he had hurt her in any way, I WOULD exact some private, one-on-one justice. I would also make sure my dad intervened in getting him expelled – assuming he was still alive.

After class, I hung back and waited for her. She finally acknowledged me. I took her arm and said, "Let's go talk." She held onto my arm as we walked which brought me such relief. It wasn't something I had done; it was something else. *"Lord, please give me Your Wisdom in this. Help me, Lord."* We went to our table in the far corner in the library behind the shelves. I said, "What is it Kristi? Has someone hurt you? Tell me everything, Kristi. I want to help."

She was still crying and my heart was hurting because she was hurting. I pulled her to me and just held her. She didn't pull away. I was so nervous. These were unchartered waters for me.

Finally she looked up at me. I said, "Honey, what can I do? Please tell me."

She said, "There's nothing you can do; there's nothing anyone can do. Why is America so evil? Why do the good people let evil people exist?"

I said, "Kristi, there's always something we can do. Please tell me. Has someone hurt you?"

"No, no one has hurt me, but I can't tell you. It's not my secret to tell. But I have to do something. He's a monster. But what can I do? – I'm just a girl still in High School. If I report it, it will cause more damage than what's been done already."

She was looking into my eyes with her tear-filled eyes searching for an answer from me. I wanted to keep holding her. I wanted to kiss her, but this was not the time or place. She just needed comforting and I wanted to be the one to do it. She must have sensed my thoughts because she turned away.

Then everything made sense from the intel mom had gathered. I turned her back to face me.

"Kristi, is it Reecy's stepfather?"

Her eyes got big with complete surprise. "How . . . how did you know?"

I couldn't tell her what I had witnessed that day, but I had seen this scenario so many times. Our family's mission was to help families who were struggling – whether from drug addiction, domestic violence, sexual abuse, child abuse, etc. We dealt with human misery in every way. We had just recently attended training for trauma victims, who weren't in need of hospitalization, where we were taught to hold the victims until they went to sleep. Much like swaddling wraps used on babies, it seemed to comfort them in a way like no other. They would still need counseling and treatment for PTSD or whatever condition brought on by the trauma, but somehow holding the victims right after the trauma seemed to have an accelerant effect on their recovery.

I explained to Kristi how my parents' mission helped people just like Reecy. I said, "Kristi, we can get her to a safe house while we arrest this pig."

Kristi said, "Yes, but her stepdad is keeping her mother drugged so he can continue to abuse her. He keeps attempting to get to her little sister. David, her sister is only six years old! To thwart him, Reecy has always intervened, but she doesn't know how long she can be successful. David, she offers herself so he won't go after her sister. He's a monster. David, what can we do?"

Again, I loved the way she said my name. She was finally looking to me for help and I knew we *could* help Reecy. But more than anything, I wanted to comfort Kristi.

"Kristi, we can get her mother into rehab. Please let me call my Mom. She has a team that handles just these types of situations."

Kristi said, "But she doesn't want to be separated from her little sister."

"I know, Kristi, we can get them all to a safe house. And she will NOT be separated from her mom or her sister, but they will be protected from their abuser. Can I call my Mom about this?"

Kristi kept searching my eyes to determine if I was telling the truth. She nodded yes.

I said, "You go back to class and don't worry about anything else. Trust me, Reecy and her little sister will have a very safe and happy Christmas . . . thanks to you."

Kristi looked up at me, wanting to believe me, but still looked doubtful. So beautiful; my heart was racing. I couldn't stop looking at her. I could tell she wanted to trust me, but still had some lingering doubt about my ability. She probably had experience with people who were all talk and no action. She just kept staring back at me, probably debating whether I could be trusted or not. One day she would completely trust my word. As she was staring, my thoughts turned from Reecy's situation to the situation I was dealing with. I wanted to kiss her more than anything. I wanted to hold her. I wanted her.

"Yes, call your Mom."

She pulled away and went to class. I watched her as she walked away and prayed that God would put what I was feeling into her heart as well. I couldn't explain what was happening to me, but I was beyond wanting to fix it.

I called Mom, explained the situation and went to class. I knew Mom would put a plan into action and Reecy's stepdad would probably be arrested by the end of the day.

I learned later that Mom had pulled Reecy out of class, counseled her on her options, taken her to the doctor at the Sanctuary, then the police station to file a report. Her stepdad was immediately arrested and jailed without bail. Mom had taken Reecy back to their apartment, packed a few personal items and her sister's toys and taken them both to a townhouse that was guarded and safe. Her mother agreed to go to rehab, which was located in the same guarded compound as Reecy's townhouse.

Since Reecy was 18, she qualified for a townhouse at the Sanctuary, a compound that my parents had designed, built and staffed, which had houses, apartments, townhouses with small yards, a 24/7 daycare, a common house with a fully-staffed kitchen and cafeteria, a small hospital and many rooms for meetings, home school and counseling along with a clothing/housing goods dispensary. The entire place was fenced with ex-military and police as security guards who lived on the premises. The entire operational expenses of the complex were funded by local churches, businesses and wealthy philanthropists in the community.

Legally, Reecy would also be custodian for her little sister. Her mom would be treated at the on-site rehab, but would not be able to visit for six months into her treatment. Reecy could have no male visitors, but as many approved female visitors as she liked. She would submit visitor names to the administration, who would run background checks on all who wanted access. Many of the employees had also been previous recipients or patients. Reecy then went to high school classes on the premises, but would be eligible to graduate with the rest of the class at Hillcrest. She would also go through counseling for sexually abused kids. My mom visited her every day bringing food, clothing, toys, school supplies, etc. Reecy loved my mom and thanked her every day for all she had done to get Reecy out of the situation. My mom told her how I had discovered Kristi crying, but Kristi had not told me who it was she was crying about. She told her that I had guessed it, so please don't be mad at Kristi. Reecy said that she owed Kristi so much and wanted to thank her somehow. I would make sure that happened.

That afternoon I sat in my Hummer just to watch her walk to the bus. She didn't even look my way. "God, please show her" I prayed.

I had the same dream that night. It took me so long to go to sleep. I kept thinking about Kristi, the looks we shared, the Christmas break coming up. Would I see her? What could I do to arrange a meeting during the Christmas break? I forgot to ask her about dinner, so maybe next weekend. But there were only three more days until the break. On Monday, I knew my assignment. The weekend wasn't a total loss because I watched a certain video over and over. OCD on steroids. Kristi Day binge watching. I loved it!

Coach Davis had other plans for me for the remaining days of school and I didn't see her once. As I was leaving Wednesday afternoon, I noticed her bus had already left. My heart was heavy.

When I got home, I dropped the cards on the table with my journal *and went to my room to pray. He would help me get through this.*

"Holy Father, I know You know what's going on – You know the beginning to the end. Will You please help me endure this? Lord, I love her so much. Why did You put her in my life? She just doesn't seem to want me like I want her? Did you want me to feel this pain? Father, am I reaping this because I've caused someone else pain like this? Please forgive me. God, please help me. I need You. I need her. Help me, Father. You said in Your Word, 'I will never leave you for forsake you. Trust in Me and lean not to your own understanding.'"

A peace came over me and I knew I could put this under the cross and He would lead me. *"Thank You JESUS!"*

When I went downstairs, Mom held out that familiar folded notebook page. I grabbed it and ran outside to read it.

"Hi David. Thank you so much for your comforting words on Friday. They really helped me deal with this situation. Can you please let me know what's going on with her? She hasn't come back to school. I don't want to put her name in this note in case this note falls into other hands. Just please keep me updated and if there's a possibility that I can visit her. I just need her address. Have a wonderful Christmas. Your family sound like wonderful people. You are a very blessed man. Your friend, Kristi."

Now where did she learn covert transmissions to prevent outing someone? Most people did not triangulate to that degree. She must have put this note in the locker on Monday. I loved her notes, but at the same time I was bothered that the note sounded so, so clinical. And the fact she always signed off as "friend." I wanted to be so much more than that to her. I loved where she said, "you are a very blessed man." So I was a man to her and not a boy. Hallelujah!

I folded the note back and put it in my pocket to put away later with her other notes to re-read and analyze for any hidden meaning in her words. Man, I had it bad.

8 DECEMBER: WEEK 4

I heard Mom calling me. When I went in, she said, "David, you need to start packing for the Spec Ops training." My heart sank. I had completely forgotten about this six-week training course. Scheduled for January 3rd through the middle of February, this was the critical six-week training operation that would determine whether I passed on to more covert and classified training or fall short (and be disqualified). There were only eleven of us (one crumbled at the last minute) that beat out about 150 others and I was the youngest one to have ever come this far. This was the operation where we parachuted into some undisclosed location and we had to survive by our own wits for six weeks! We could take any supplies we could carry in one pack – except guns and ammunition.

I had looked forward to this training all year, but I didn't want to leave now because for six weeks I wouldn't be there to tell her my feelings or protect her – and a lot could happen in six weeks.

There was too much going on – with Sasha's daily torments, Richie hanging around her, Zach and even Russell could try to move in again. I had to come up with a plan. *"Holy Father, please show me what I need to do to insure that Kristi is protected. Please send Your warrior angels to protect her while I'm gone. Thank You, Father, for answering my prayers."*

Rats and snakes were the most common things people ate on these survival trainings, but I asked God to provide for me that I would not be reduced to eating that! Most guys came back dehydrated and dangerously skinny, and probably full of worms. Beyond that, we were to also capture a displayed flag from each trainee's camp. That meant we had to track each man to his camp and take the flag somehow. My heart sank deeper into despair when I realized I wouldn't see her again until February! God, HELP ME! Maybe I could use that time to get her out of my brain! Except, truthfully, I didn't want to get her out of my brain. I decided to get her a Christmas card and write an explanation about Reecy. I would have Mom mail it on Monday. Then I prayed about what God wanted me to pack in my backpack for the training. That night I had a dream of everything I needed to take. He was always so faithful. *Thank You JESUS!*

I had packed all my light-weight supplies – light pan, telescoping cups, camouflage tarp, netting, colloidal silver soap. Added to this I packed three, 24-inch pieces of rebar, MMS drops to purify water. I also packed some in a spray for bug bites, etc. MMS also killed any pathogen, bacteria or virus in the body and could be used to cure malaria. Big pharma had suppressed its healing properties for many years. I knew everything the Lord had led me to take would be used.

Now what could I do to protect Kristi while I was away? I called one of my best friends, Stephan, and told him that I had some personal matters to take care of and I wouldn't be back until the middle of February. I asked him to look after Kristi and I stressed that this was not a casual assignment. I explained that she was being targeted by several bullies and I wanted him make this his main priority while I was gone. If he had to skip classes or be late, it would be excused. I suspected that he knew I had more power around that School than most people were aware of, but he had the training to keep his mouth shut. Also, since his workout schedule was even more intense than mine and he was several inches taller and many pounds heavier, he could take anyone, maybe two or three in a fight.

I stressed strongly how important this was to me and he accepted this assignment and I knew he would loyally perform this task. I think he may have known I wasn't going to any fluff seminar, but he had the good sense not to question me about it. He was a great friend and warrior when it came to defending the defenseless.

I saw Kristi as she was walking down the hall and I headed straight towards her when suddenly, Richie appeared out of nowhere. She looked at him and smiled. He put his arm around her as he walked away with her. I was trying to scream, "Kristi, Kristi," but my mouth wouldn't go above a whisper. I couldn't let this happen. I had never told her how I felt. I tried again to call but my voice was barely audible. Suddenly I woke with a start – wide awake. It had been a dream. Thank God. She wasn't with Richie. Would that still be the case when I returned? Was this a premonition? All I could do was pray.

My heart was so heavy. Why did she continually reject me? I wanted to tell her that I would go to Africa with her and help her with the mission. She needed to know that. She needed me to help her. I would put that in the note with my Christmas card. *"God, please help me with this. Your Word said to acknowledge You in all my ways, and You will give me the desires of my heart. Lord, you know how much I want her. And I know You have led me to her. Please show her, Lord. I love You."*

I found the perfect Christmas card. It read: "Christmas means many things to many people, but to most CHRISTians, it celebrates the birth of the One who died for them." I loved it. Even though we didn't believe that Jesus was born on December 25th (shepherds wouldn't have been in the field in the winter and the time to register with the government in Israel was in September or early October), it was a time to remind people that Jesus was real and we needed to be ready for His return. Hallelujah! It was a big card, so I had plenty of room to write.

"Kristi, this note may surprise you, but I want you to know that I have been praying a lot about what you told me after my speech. You were right. I have asked God to reveal HIS direction for my life and I have had incredible revelation on this – and it involves helping you in Africa. That's why I wanted to talk to you the other day. I wanted to tell you the details and have you pray over it to see what God is telling you. My mother has also been praying and getting the same messages I've gotten.

Oh, and Reecy and Bethany are very safe and happy. I will let my mom fill you in on that situation. Reecy wants to thank you. She credits you with saving her life, her sister's life and her mother's life. Oh, and her stepfather is in jail without bail. I won't go into detail, but there was irrefutable evidence of his guilt, so he is looking at some serious jail time.

Please let me know when we can talk. Let me take you to dinner, then afterwards, we can come to my house so we can have some privacy when we talk. My parents want to meet you as well.

I have to be in training for the next six weeks, so this should give you time to pray, seek our Holy Father's Will, and get the message He sends you. I will be praying for you while I'm gone. I will be missing you as well. You have come to mean a great deal to me. God bless you, my dear, dear Kristi. ~David"

I put the Card in the back of my journal. I would give it to Mom to mail on Monday.

I envisioned her reading the card, then going to her room to pray about it. The Lord would show her exactly what He had shown me. She would pray for me and think about me every day while I was gone. I wanted to just hold her. How could any one person have so much power over someone else's feelings? This was almost too much to bear, but I would gladly wait in order to get back to civilization and hopefully into her arms as we were meant to be. Yes, when I got back, we would both be on the same page. She would miss me so much, of that I was certain. I imagined that when I returned, she would run to me, put her arms around my neck and kiss me. I thought of that happy scenario over and over. *"God, please help her see. Guide her to everything You've shown me. Thank You, Holy Father."*

9 JANUARY

Kristi's Journal – January

I was glad Christmas was over. We didn't really celebrate Christmas; it was so commercial and people weren't really talking about Jesus – the reason for the season. My parents didn't have much money anyway. Sometimes I had enough money for lunch and sometimes not. The refrigerator seemed to stay bare now. It was something no one talked about, which was so odd because my parents had always included me in whatever circumstances we found ourselves in. I felt unable to help and I didn't press the lunch money because I didn't want to add to their burdens.

I had not heard back from David about Reecy and I couldn't wait to get back to school to find out about her. I really liked David. I know Sasha was in love with him and I overheard all she said about their "make out" sessions. For some reason, she made sure that I heard it – in graphic detail. I tried to get my books as quickly as possible so I wouldn't have to hear more. It hurt my heart to hear those things. I really liked him. I knew, given the right circumstances, I could probably love him. What a shame. He was such a fine young man – but defiled. He was so handsome – too handsome for his own good, but he had such a sweet and compassionate nature to him. And he did love Jesus. I really liked being with him, but I would not come between him and Sasha. Why would someone like David allow himself to be so taken in by a flirt like Sasha? But that was not my business. God had always used flawed people. Even David in the Bible was flawed, but God had promised me a husband who was not defiled and I was holding Him to that promise. I didn't know when or how, but I DID know that God was faithful. *"Thank You, JESUS!"*

* * * * * * *

I had packed everything the Lord had led me to pack. Some things didn't make sense, but I obeyed. Obedience is better than sacrifice. I just kept praying, begging that I would not have to eat rats. I loved great food, but rat was not on the menu! If all else failed, I would simply fast. I had done a 21-day fast before, but never a six-week fast. I lucked out, though, because the first two weeks we trained almost continuously, pounding out push-ups, timed runs, cold ocean plunges, heavy lifting and a battery of mind games with the ubiquitous screaming, but we were well fed during those two weeks, so I really only had to survive for four weeks. The entire goal of this training was to survive – by whatever means necessary!

They were preparing us for wherever they were dropping us. Somehow I knew we were going somewhere tropical and I packed accordingly. I was not wrong – the Lord had guided me. When we were circling what looked like an island, the commander jerked me up by my parachute straps and forced me up next to him. I expected to be jumping first, but he wanted me there to help facilitate the process. In other words, I was to push them out. I heard in my spirit, *"Look where they're landing."* And *"Look at the layout of the island."* I was in the perfect position and obeyed. Until I looked at my compass, I still couldn't tell the directions, but that wouldn't be a problem long. After we had almost flown the entire island, I was pushed out. *I started praying, "Father, please let me land in a great place."* Floating to the landing, I flew over the palm trees and spotted the beach. I maneuvered the parachute with the winds into landing almost in the water and the softest part of the sand. The landing was perfect and my parachute was salvageable and could be used for many other things. Most guys got caught up in trees and had to cut the parachute loose. *"Thank You JESUS!"* God was so good to me.

I knew I had to set up camp quickly before the sun went down. I stuffed my chute in my backpack and started walking to the trees. I said, *"Lord, please show me where I need to set up."* The Word says *"Walk in the Spirit and you will not fulfill the lusts of the flesh. Lean not to your own understanding. Trust in the Lord."* I thought of verse after verse and these comforted me. About that time, I stepped on what I thought was solid ground, but it gave way and I realized I was sliding down a steep embankment. I then started rolling and finally ended up on a huge rock jutting out of the side of the hill I had just fallen down. My backpack had cushioned the fall. I looked up to where I had fallen from and could only see thick vegetation. I heard the sound of a small waterfall nearby and knew it was probably fresh water. But I was surrounded by lush vegetation that I would have to get out of. How did I get in this mess? *"God, please help me."* I went around to the other side of the rock which was also covered in thick vegetation. For some reason, I pulled aside the heavy vegetation. I looked and I couldn't believe it. That vegetation was covering up an entrance to a cave just big enough for me to crawl through. I knew this was from God. *Thank You Jesus!*

I parted the thick bushes and peeked inside. I had to crawl through the small opening, but then the cave opened up inside so much that I could stand up and not hit my head. It was perfectly dry and unoccupied which was another relief. This would be perfect. I took out my compass and discovered I was at the south end of the island – just as I had hoped. With the prevailing winds, any smoke I created would be blown out to sea. I gathered wood and started a fire. I had put rocks around the fire pit so I could place my rebar on top that would hold my pan. I noticed the smoke from the fire was being sucked further into the cave, so there must have been air movement to the outside and the smoke would be somewhat dissipated. Then I could cook my Spam and eat right out of the pan. I took inventory of the precious Spam I had packed. No rats tonight! *Thank You JESUS*! I only had room for a few Spam containers and that certainly wouldn't last four weeks. Then I realized that God HAD answered my prayers. He had given me the perfect camping spot, so I knew He would provide food also. It wasn't dark yet, but I took a nap anyway. Had that same dream about Jesus. Then I had dreams about her. I relived every single time I had been with her; every look we had shared and every conversation we had ever had. I especially liked to relive the times I had touched her. Maybe that's what I needed to do to get her out of my system – just think about her 24/7. I would get tired of it eventually. She was before me. Jesus was before me. Jesus, holding my hand, put me on the rock and smiled at me. Sweet sleep engulfed me.

I woke with a start, but then began to realize I was not in my warm clean bed. It was 3:00am by my watch that auto-adjusted to location. I was wide awake. "*Lord, what do you want me to do?*" I heard in my spirit – *"Go get some flags, son!"* Then I remembered where each soldier had landed, so they wouldn't be too far to hike to. They would all be very tired from having to work to set up camp, whereas my camp had been supernaturally set up and I had been able to take a nap, so my energy would be high for nocturnal missions.

I remembered seeing a cleared-off area to the west where some of the guys had jumped. Exiting the cave, I said, *"Lord, which way should I go?"* Then a firefly lit up to my left, so I followed it. It eventually flew off but I instinctively knew where to go. I must have hiked several miles before the clearing. From my position, I somehow also KNEW where the camps were. Getting into stealth mode, I skirted the outside of the clearing until I noticed the tell-tale signs of brush being used to cover tracks. I moved the brush and followed the tracks. There it was and I knew my comrade was sleeping. Now where was that flag? "Lord, where is that flag?" Then I saw it stuck in a helmet next to his head. This might be tricky. When I got closer, he started snoring so loudly I thought he would wake up. I took the flag and started backing away.

"*Okay, Lord, where is the next flag?"* I felt led to keep going west. I came to the other camp. The flag had been tied to a booby-trapped tree, so I just cut the rope, put a broken stick in where the flag had been, and tied the string back the way he had it for the booby-trap. What a joke. This seemed so easy. *"Thank You JESUS!"*

I got two more flags, then decided to call it a night. It was starting to get light anyway and I had to make it back to my camp. If I could capture two more flags, though, I would be the default winner. I said, *"Lord, can I go back now?"* and a peace came over me and I knew I had His Blessing. He had been faithful and answered my prayers. He was my strong tower in the day of trouble. *"I love You, Father. I love You, Jesus. I love You, Holy Spirit."* Kristi was so right: I AM a blessed man. *"God, please protect her."* I kept replaying the video of her in my mind and I imagined her reaction when she saw me when I got home. That's when she would kiss me because she loved me. Hallelujah!

I went back to the cave and slept the entire next day. I decided not to go anywhere that night, so I just prayed. Visions of Kristi followed me everywhere; my every thought. *"Father, please look after her. Send Your warrior angels to guard her and I plead the BLOOD OF JESUS over her."* I wish I had a picture of her, but I had her in my mind thanks to the OCD video marathons. I especially remembered her almost in my arms. And the times she had put her hand in mine; the time I was walking towards her in the hall when she was talking and laughing with Bryan. So beautiful. I missed her. *"God, please help me."*

I finished the rest of my Spam, so I knew I had to go shopping for food. Where would it be? Publix? Walmart? Rat-ville? I said, *"Okay, Lord, can you please show me where I can get some food?"* This time I was led east. I walked and walked. I had found fresh water near the cave, but had already depleted my canteen. I would have to turn back if I didn't find something soon. Then I heard people talking. What was this? Getting on my belly, I slithered to the edge of their camp. This was where the officers were camping! I didn't know they were even on the island.

Well what do you know? I smelled the steaks being cooked. No rats for them. They were laughing at us having to eat rats and who knows what else. They were also drinking – a lot – and cussing and talking about women – and not in a respectful way. Why did some guys have to be so crude? I just nestled in and waited for the inevitable. Their camp was so far from the others, I'm sure they felt they didn't even need a guard posted. After about four hours, I could tell a drunken stupor had taken hold of them all because of the snoring and complete silence.

I slipped under the back wall of the mess tent and went shopping. I grabbed the cooler with the steaks – ALL of them! Then I grabbed a bag full of potatoes – enough to feed an army. If they had had a flag, I would have taken that too. Now I was really weighted down and I knew any footprints would be easily followed.

I said, *"Lord, what do I do now?"* Then I heard water bubbling down the rocks from a stream. Walking further away from their camp, I came to a shallow stream that I knew was the same stream that led near my cave. I tied a chute cord around the cooler (which floated) and put the potatoes on top of the cooler. Then I waded down the stream with the cooler attached. They certainly wouldn't be able to trace footprints in water. After about 30 minutes, the water was getting almost too deep for me and I knew I needed to get back on land.

"Father, will You guide me out of here?" I then heard in my spirit. *"Look under the brush to your right."* I waded over and found an intact bamboo raft! Wow. Who could have made this? A former rat eater? The stream was chest-high now but with the raft, I could simply float down the river with my stash. *"Thank You LORD! You are so good to me."*

I floated for almost two hours when I came to the same area where I had placed my totally natural-looking markers. I pulled the raft out of the water and took my stash to my cave. No one would see these footprints unless they fell down the same ravine I did.

I stoked up the cave fire again and had one of the best meals I've ever had. I had even discovered a stash of real butter at the bottom if the steak cooler and cookies! I just felt bad for the other guys. I made a note to place some potatoes around each camp and share my bounty as I captured their flags. I leaned back and remembered again how she had looked up at Bryan and smiled so sweetly. The day I caught her before she fell. She held me so tight. I know it wasn't me; she had been frightened, so she held onto me. But one day – probably my first day back – she would hold me because she wanted to. I was nodding out, but sort of trying to stay awake because I wanted to keep her in my mind. I fell before Him but He held out His hand to me. I took His hand. My Jesus. Sweet sleep engulfed me.

* * * * * * *

Kristi's Journal – January

Where IS he? No one seems to know where he went. Did he transfer to a different school? His locker has not been touched. I want to ask Sasha, but I know I would be at the mercy of her abuse if I did. Bryan didn't know either. He didn't even have David's cell phone number. I am so worried about Reecy. What have I done? Did my confession to David hurt her in any way? "Lord, please show me she's okay."

I went to the school office to ask about Reecy, but they "were not at liberty to discuss the matter." That sounded so ominous. *"God, wherever she is, please help her."* I felt in my heart that my interference had caused great harm to come to her and her family. I thought I could trust David. Please forgive me if this was my fault that any harm has come to her. Did my confession to David cause her to be separated from her family? My heart ached so with that thought. *Please put it on David's heart to contact me. Thank You Father.*

My heart is breaking for her. And there was that weird Stephan guy again. What was HE doing here? Why would he be lurking in the hall just watching me? Heading to my next class, I picked up my pace to get away from him.

10 FEBRUARY

Kristi's Journal – February

I went to the office to find out how I could graduate early. I do not like being here at all. Since my speech, people were much nicer to me, but they kept their distance. Bryan is still friendly and Stephan seems to be hanging around me everywhere. He always sits a few tables away at lunch and I catch him looking at me. He never speaks, just hovers. It is so strange. Once I saw him talking to Zach, Larry and Dean, but they haven't really bothered me at all. *Thank You Jesus!*

I asked the school counselor what the steps were for early graduation and she gave me the procedures list, so maybe I can finish up in early April and graduate with the rest of the class in late May. I wouldn't attend; I just wanted that piece of paper for my parents. I asked Principal O'Reilly about Reecy. He is so nice, but he won't give me any info about her either. That whole situation is such a burden to me. I feel so bad for what I did. I trusted the wrong person. Why had he lied? The hurt I felt for Reecy was compounded by my having trusted an unfaithful person. When will I learn?

As I left Principal O'Reilly's office, my eyes were filled with tears thinking about what I had done to Reecy. I opened the door to the hall and stumbled right into Stephen's arms! He held me so I wouldn't fall. What was he doing here? Had he followed me?

Instinctively, I said, "I'm so sorry." Looking into my eyes, he said, "It's not a problem. Are you okay?" I pulled away from him and said, "Yes, I'm fine. Thank you." I hurried away. Turning into class, I looked back only to discover that he was still behind me. He *had* followed me. This is so scary and David is no longer here to intercept. *"God, please send Your angels to protect me. Thank You Father."*

* * * * * * *

After a few weeks of living in the cave, I asked the Lord to show me another place with plenty of sunshine. We had had a few bad storms and the cave was great protection and I could always go back if necessary because that was where my stash was kept. I was just getting tired of sleeping on the hard ground. I wanted somewhere with a view and sunshine! I started walking down the ravine, but felt led to turn around and go back up the same hill I had fallen down. I was between the beach and the stream, but kept walking.

At the top of a hill, I came to a grove of tropical trees which were tall, straight and had a canopy of foliage near the top. The problem was there were no branches except near the top. I came to one of the trees in the middle of the grove and touched the tree. This may sound strange, but that tree was "telling" me to choose it. I decided to climb it. Fortunately, I had been led to pack some tree climbing boot attachments. I strapped those on, doubled some chute cord, wrapped it around the tree and started climbing. I could easily rappel down. This was a very tall tree and almost hidden from any view because it was in the middle of the thicket. When I got to the top I found a huge bird nest. I could not possibly have seen this from the ground, so I KNEW the Lord had led me to this tree. *"Thank You LORD!"*

It looked like an abandoned eagle's nest, but I didn't even know if eagles were indigenous to the area. Whatever bird it was, it was big. I got in the middle of the soft nest and KNEW this was where the Lord had led me. It was even slanted up like an inclined bed. I thought of Psalm 91. *He shall cover me with His feathers and under His wings shall I trust.* I served a great big GOD! Hallelujah! I had captured two more flags and left steaks and potatoes as a rat-free consolation prize. I also left "presents" at the other camps for taking their flags. I knew that by this time, these guys were needing some fat.

I was getting stronger and more ripped by the day and hadn't had to consume rat one! *"Thank You JESUS!"* I was simply amazed at how the Lord had led me in almost every decision. *"God, thank YOU for all of these directions. But, Lord, You know what I really want. I want her. Father, please show me what to do."* Thoughts of her were filling my mind continually. It was easy to think that I was succeeding because of my strength, but it was the strength of Jesus. *Be strong in the Lord and the power of His might.* Thank You LORD! Thoughts of her also kept me emotionally stable. I couldn't wait to see her.

I left the food in the cave, blocking the entrance with a rock, and carried my sleeping gear and supplies to my nest. I used my chute to cover the inside of the nest and I had packed one camouflage tarp in case it rained. I used a bamboo pole to prop up my netting. If it rained I could put the tarp over it, with the sides draping over the nest, so whatever runoff there was would fall to the ground. I rappelled back to the ground and looked from every angle to see if there was an indication of a "camp." Not one. Even if you were directly under the nest, you still couldn't see it. Yes, I served a great big GOD! Hallelujah!

* * * * * * *

Kristi's Journal:

I had stayed behind to talk to Miss Jenkins about the requirements for taking the accelerated classes for early graduation. I had study period scheduled anyway, so I could go to the Library any time. She is so nice and such a different kind of teacher than Mr. Watkins. The halls were pretty much deserted when I left. As I reached for the handle of the fire doors to the stairs, Zach appeared out of nowhere and blocked the door. He grabbed my arms and pushed me against the wall. Then he tried to push me into the hidden area around the corner. I knew I couldn't let him succeed. Suddenly, he pushed me backwards into someone who was lurking in that area. My back was pressed up against his hard chest. He was very tall and very large. His huge arm immediately wrapped around my waist. I completely froze and closed my eyes. Fear gripped me. There was no way I could escape now. All I could do was pray. He was holding me so close and I was backed completely into his chest. What would this person do to me? I knew I couldn't fight TWO big guys. I was so scared; my heart was beating so fast, but I was silently praying. *"God, please help me."*

Then he spoke. I heard, "Zach, does harassing a much smaller person make you feel like a big man? I've already warned you once. You must not know that I don't give second warnings."

My eyes flew open. It was Stephen and he was still holding onto me! He was protecting me! I looked at Zach. The blood had drained out of his face and I realized he was petrified of Stephen.

More scared than I was.

He said, “Hey, man. We were just playing. Kristi loves this. Don’t you Kristi?”

Stephen said, “Is that true, Kristi? Do you like Zach bullying you and trying to hurt you?”

Still filled with terror but looking directly at Zach, I said, “No, I don’t.”

“Well, there you go, Zach. I think you heard her.” Zach started backing away. Stephen said, “Oh, and if I catch you bothering her again, trust me, people won’t be able to recognize you for a long, long time. Do you understand me?”

Meekly, Zach said, “Yeah, man. No harm done.” All three started backing further away.

“Get out of here, you scum.” All three shot off down the hall.

Relief flooded me. I was safe. God had used Stephen to help me. I turned to Stephen. He had just saved me, but I was still trembling all over. Flooded with relief, emotion overtook me and I threw my arms around his neck. I was so grateful. Holding onto him, with my head still spinning with confusion, I just whispered, “Oh David.”

Gently pushing me back, holding me at arms’ length and looking into my eyes, he said, “Stephen.”

What had I just done? Called this brave man another man’s name. There was such a gentle look in his eyes. He said, “Zach won’t be bothering you again.” He dropped his hold and stepped back.

Feeling so guilty for misjudging him and calling him David, I said, “Stephen?”

He stopped and turned back to face me but said nothing.

“Thank you. . . . Thank you for helping me. I don’t know what I would have done.”

“It was my pleasure, Kristi. He won’t bother you again. I’ll see to it.”

With that, he picked up my book bag, handed it to me, then took my arm. He said, “Now, let’s get you to the Library” and we continued up the stairs. Stopping at the door he said, “God bless you, Kristi.”

How did he know my next class was study period? *“Holy Father, please forgive me for judging him. Thank You, LORD, that he is a Christian. I had no idea. You had sent him to me. Thank You LORD!”* Immediately, a thought came to me that David had sent Stephen to help me. I then pushed that thought away. David didn’t care about me; I wasn’t in that special group that he and Sasha belonged to. He had abandoned me.

Update: Zach has not been back at school all week. There is a rumor that he has been beaten up by someone and he’s staying out to let his face heal. *God, please help him. Open his eyes Lord. Let him see that Jesus is the only way to You.*

* * * * * * *

Half a world away, David had an urgent need to pray for Kristi. *“Father, please send Your angels to protect her.”* He kept praying and prayed that Stephen had everything under control. He would give anything to know what was going on with her.

Two more weeks and I would be home. I still kept having the dream of Jesus and I still loved Kristi with all my heart. I now knew without a doubt that she was the one God had chosen for me. I would not waver. As soon as I got back, I knew she would know also. God would show her as He had shown me. A peace came over me and I knew God would lead me in every step of my life. I had brought along a small notebook and I began a NEW 5-10 year plan. I decided Kristi was right and I would not go into ministry. I would go with her to Africa and I couldn't wait to get back to her to see what the Lord had shown her. Jesus had called me long ago and I was already doing His Work. I would follow His lead in every decision in life and would do His Will – with GOD's blessing. *Thank You JESUS!*

* * * * * *

February 17th

It was a cold Tuesday morning when I walked back into school. Everyone greeted me like I was a returning conqueror (which, technically, was true). I looked in all the usual places for Kristi, but she wasn't around. Lord, where is she? I checked the attendance several times to make sure she was here today. I had to spend the next few days in the Testing Lab studying makeup modules because I had missed so many classes. I felt her presence, though. Surely, she knew I was back. I wanted to hold her and I couldn't wait to see her face when she saw me. When class modules were completed, I knew Kristi's bus had already left, so I just went to my locker. My heart was so heavy; I wanted to just hold her and finally see that she shared my feelings. Hopefully the Christmas card made my intentions very clear. If I knew her better, I would drive to her house, but we had not reached that point yet. My main goal for tomorrow would be to find her and tell her even more of what the Lord was showing me!

Opening my locker, the first thing I saw was a printed photo on top of everything else. It was a picture of Kristi with her arms wrapped around Stephen's neck. My heart sank. THIS was why she was avoiding me! She was with Stephen now. I had to hand it to Stephen. He had done his job above and beyond anything I could have imagined. What kind of loyalty was that? I felt so betrayed – both by Stephan AND Kristi. A pure rage was coursing through me. Because of his protection, I imagined, she had fallen in love with him. I knew that most guys in this School were already in love with her. I was livid. Trying to control my anger, I speed-dialed his cell.

Answering, he said, "Hey man. What's up? I heard you were back."

"Stephen" I said. "I'm at my locker. Get over here right now." and hung up.

Within minutes, he was standing in front of me. It took every ounce of restraint not to beat the hell out of him. I handed him the picture. "What the hell is this?"

He laughed and started explaining in detail what had happened that day with Zach. He told me that when she was backed into him, she started trembling head to toe. She was so scared because she didn't know who she had backed into.

"But David, you're the one she loves. While she was hugging me because she was so grateful that I had just saved her from a possible rape, the very moment the cretin took this picture, she called me 'David'."

Relief and confusion flooded over me. My friend, Stephen, had saved her. She loved me? I just looked at Stephen in disbelief. "What? You mean you didn't encourage this?" Then realizing the full weight of what he was saying, I said, "Wait . . . she did?"

"Yeah, man. You don't have anything to worry about. I don't blame you; I could easily fall for her, but she loves you and I would never try to come between what you two have! But you were right. This girl is being bullied like you wouldn't believe. I tailed her as soon as she got off the bus until she got back on. I watched everything she has to go through every day. I really don't see how she can handle the constant attacks. Believe me, the average Christian could not withstand the perpetual onslaught that she tolerates every day. Actually, a hardened Marine couldn't withstand what she goes through. After tailing her for a few days, though, it got better for her because everyone knew I was looking out for her and they backed off. I had a serious talk with a few people – including Zach and friends."

"Really? I had no idea. I've not seen her being bullied to that degree – just Sasha and Zach."

"That's because when you're around, everyone is on their best behavior. David, you just don't realize what a positive effect you have on others."

Still reeling from his previous revelation, I said, "Are you serious? Why is that?"

"Because they don't want to be on the receiving end of your anger. Plus, your walk with Jesus raises the bar for all of us. You make us want to be better men."

I was overcome with humility and confusion and, yes, pride for my faith in Jesus.

"Stephen, please forgive me. I know you've got my back and I really appreciate your looking after Kristi for me. Actually, Stephen, you saved two people that day. If he had hurt her, I would have killed him. So, brother, I owe you. Big time."

Stephen put his arm around my shoulder. "David, you are one lucky guy. She is one of a kind and has one of the sweetest spirits I've ever encountered. I turn her back over to your care." He made his way out the door and I headed to Samson with too many thoughts bombarding my brain.

I opened the back of my Hummer still reeling with his information. Stephen had gone above and beyond and I would see to it that he would be driving a new Ford truck before the week was out. She had called him my name. She DID love me. *Thank You Jesus!* Maybe that card did the trick.

Feeling on top of the world again, I started organizing my supplies. I could live in my truck from my supply stash – the mobile bug-out bag. The weather would be getting warmer soon and my stash changed accordingly.

I started thinking about the six weeks I had just endured. The training had been an incredible success for me. I had captured all ten flags and was the youngest recipient of the coveted Dominus Maximus Award and the only person to have captured all ten flags. The officers, who all looked noticeably slimmer than when they first arrived, asked everyone about the stolen food, but, true to the code of ethics, no one said a word. I knew they knew it was me because of the "gifts" I had left and the fact that I had captured all the flags. We all just gave each other knowing looks and they all congratulated me privately on the success. If they only knew that ALL of my success was because I had listened to HIS voice. *My sheep hear My voice and another they will not follow.* Hallelujah!

I was later "interviewed" by the officers to give detailed accounts of how I survived. I also wouldn't want them to be able to circumvent the skills of the next McGyver to come along. Most exit interviews lasted about an hour, but mine dragged out for two hours! I wasn't about to give them the details and the miraculous ways that God had led me every step of the way. They wouldn't understand. I had come back more ripped and "Marine-like" than ever before. I couldn't wait to see her.

Smiling within I kept thinking 'she called him my name.' I heard a sound. Still in training mode, I immediately got into defense stance and turned around. It was Kristi! I could only stare at her. Would she throw her arms around me like she had with Stephen? I stepped towards her but she made no move to hold me and instead, moved back a few steps. I had waited for this moment for over six weeks, but now that it was here, I was completely speechless. Why wasn't she running into my arms? I was also shocked that she had been able to walk up on me without my hearing her. Her stealth training seemed superior to guys I trained with. Looking directly into those beautiful eyes, I realized how vulnerable I was – physically and emotionally. Suddenly I couldn't breathe very well and for once, I didn't know what to do. I wanted to hold her, to kiss her, but I held back until I knew she was sharing my feelings.

She looked worried and almost angry about something.

She looked so pained. What had happened? She said, "I thought you had transferred to another school. Nobody knew where you were."

I stammered, "No . . . no, I had to attend some training, but I couldn't find you to tell you."

Trying to hold her anger, she said, "I just want to know what happened to Reecy. I've been so worried and you left and didn't say anything. I know what I told you has caused her great harm."

She was really anxious now and no longer held back her anger at me. "I've tried to find her; I went to her apartment. No one knew anything. No one would tell me anything when I went to the school office. No one would tell me what happened to her. I didn't know what to do. Where were you? Why would you just leave me not knowing what happened to her? Why would you DO that to me? I thought you were my friend."

She was talking so fast and she was so upset. Then I realized I had never mailed the card. How could I have forgotten something so important? So many thoughts were blasting through my mind. I could see she was worried – but not about me. She had been dominant in my thoughts almost every waking minute, all my dreams, all my imaginings and she had not even missed me – and was now clearly angry at me. I had never seen her angry at anyone. Why me? Why wasn't she reaching for me like she had Stephen? She had called him my name. Then it hit me. She just didn't share my feelings. Now I was hurt. More than hurt. I was furious! Hell hath no fury as a man scorned.

I couldn't take looking at her profound disappointment in me – her eyes searching mine. I turned back to my truck to hide my increasing anger and heartbreak, but she grabbed my sleeve. When she did that, the guerilla training in me surfaced. Something in me snapped. I grabbed her arm, twisted it behind her back and held her there, pulling her into me. I was gripping her hard, but not hurting her – just constraining her. She was so close to me, I wanted her now more than ever. I kept looking into her eyes, hoping for some kind of reciprocal feeling. There was nothing but anger and hurt. This was so painful, but I was still madly in love and filled with so many conflicting emotions.

Turning red with rage, she tried pulling away. She was much stronger than I had imagined. She kept struggling, pulling away and fighting me, but that only made me want to further dominate her.

"How dare you. Let me go. Stop this. Stop! Let me go. You're just like the others."

She was ripping my heart out with everything she said. She tried to wrest away, but my grip was too tight. I knew it was wrong, but I loved that she was at least showing some emotion from a situation I had complete control over. She kept fighting to get free. Then I tightened even more and pulled her closer. I tried to kiss her. She wrenched her head away and like a wounded rabbit, cried "Nooooo. Stop this. David, I said stop. I hate you. You're just a brute."

I couldn't believe those words. Hadn't she been longing to see me? She had called him my name! She had been in my every thought. Rage went through me. Most girls would willingly kiss me and a few had tried. I could have any girl I wanted, but I wanted

THIS one! I could feel every inch of her body crushed against mine. Dark thoughts went through my mind. Something happened to me when she was trying to get away from me. I wanted to hurt her. My heart was breaking and I wanted her to feel the same pain she was causing me. I tightened my grip on her arm and pulled her even closer. At that point, she went completely limp in my arms. She started to cry. For a brief moment I was glad she was crying.

Her mouth so close to mine, she whispered, "Please, David. You're hurting me." I melted at the gentleness in her voice.

Then I realized what I had been doing. Some evil force had entered me to do this to her. I was no better than Zach or Chance or even Sasha. I was immediately filled with remorse. I had gripped her with the same strength I would use on any man. I could have easily caused a lot of damage. Pain and remorse flooded me. I let go. She immediately backed away.

It felt like someone had kicked me in the gut. Now, I was almost crying.

"Kristi, I'm so sorry. I don't know what came over me. Please, PLEASE forgive me. I wouldn't hurt you for anything in the world."

She just stood there looking at me confused with tears running down her face. She had stepped far enough away that she could run if needed.

"Kristi, please forgive me."

Rubbing her arm, blinking back her tears, she looked at me with complete mistrust and hurt.

"I . . . I just want to know what happened to her; where she is."

How could I have done something like this? Minutes before I had been fantasizing of how she would run into my arms, expecting her to have missed me as much as I missed her. Now, with my brutality, I may have turned her against me forever. *"God, please help me."*

Then I knew what I had to do. I reached for her hand, but she pulled away, so I just stood before her and held out my hand, willing her in my mind to not reject me.

Pleading with her now, I said, "Come with me."

Backing further away, she said, "I'm not going anywhere with you."

"I thought you wanted to see Reecy?"

She kept rubbing her arm where I had held it. My heart filled again with remorse. I knew there would be bruises.

Calmer now, she said, "I do . . . but if you just give me her address, I will find her myself."

I could tell she just wanted to get away from me. Who could blame her? The pain I was feeling from what I had done was almost too much. I wanted to hold her; I wanted her to forgive me and trust me like she had before I had done this horrible thing. *God, please help me. I've messed this up. I need You.*

Trying not to show the sinking emotion engulfing me, I said, "Kristi, they won't let you in without someone with clearance to enter."

I could tell she didn't believe me. She looked at me in total disbelief and said, "And you have this special clearance?" almost mocking me.

"Yes." I explained. "This is my parents' mission. But there are strict rules to follow. I have to follow them like everyone else. Let me take you. I will wait while you visit and then take you home."

Still searching my eyes for some semblance of trust, she said, "I may be a while. You would wait for me?" She had already missed her bus and didn't want to walk home.

"Of course I would wait for you." (If she only knew I would wait as long as it took.) I just wanted her to trust me again.

Still looking at me, not trusting anything I said, nodded yes.

I held out my hand again, but she ignored it and walked to the truck. I opened the passenger door for her but the Hummer's modified design, with just a bar for a step, made it impossible for her to climb. I lifted her onto the seat and buckled her in. She sat in silence as we drove, looking out the window and rubbing her arm. I gave her my cell phone to call her parents and to take her mind off the pain in her arm.

"Hi momma. I'm on my way to see Reecy. David Everett is taking me. He knows where she is and I want to make sure she and her little sister are okay. Don't wait supper; I will be home later. I love you momma."

I loved the way she called her mother, "momma." Just like a little girl. My heart was still hurting. I kept praying.

"Kristi, I had a card for you, but I forgot to mail it. It explained everything about Reecy, her sister and her mom – that they're all safe and cared for. Her mom is in rehab at the same facility. I am so sorry. All this time I've been away, I thought you had read it. I meant to give it to Mom before I left."

She had no response and we drove in silence until we got to the gate. The entire time we drove in silence, I kept telling her in my mind: "I love you Kristi. Please forgive me. I love you."

The guard recognized me and waved us through. I pulled up just out of sight of Reecy's townhouse, but I could see her going down her walk with her little sister.

I said, "There she is, Kristi."

Kristi said, "She looks different."

"Well, I wouldn't know, but I know she's gone through a lot of positive changes. She will fill you in."

"Why are you parking so far away?"

"Well, because of what she's been through, men aren't allowed within a 500-yard radius, but we're a lot closer than that. They won't make me move. But I can visit in another few months I think."

"Oh, so you're not going in with me?"

"No, but I will wait for you. Stay as long as you like. I've got plenty of studying to do anyway." In reality, I was just happy to have her near me. That intense pain was still in my gut. How could I have hurt her so? *God, please help me*.

I went around to help her down. I gently lifted her and put her on the ground. I held her for a few seconds, but she pulled away, not even looking at me. She reached for her book bag, but I said, "You can leave that here if you like." I knew that mysterious journal was in that bag. Would I read it? I honestly didn't know. I tried to remember the date we were in the Library. Would my name be there?

She looked up at me finally and said, "You won't leave me?"

I could tell she wanted to trust me again, but I would have to prove myself.

"No, Kristi. I will never leave you." (If she only knew how much I meant that statement.)

She gave me an odd look, but started walking towards Reecy's. As she turned to go up her walk, she looked back at me. I prayed, *"God, please show her."*

* * * * * * *

I knocked on Reecy's door and she flung it open. "KRISTI!" she yelled. She grabbed me and hugged me and held me tightly. "I am so happy to see you."

"Reecy, I was so worried about you. I didn't know how to find you. I went to your old apartment. No one would tell me where you were. You look so different. What happened to your hair? What happened to your tattoos?"

"Oh, that. They were fake. And I just let my hair go back to the natural color and took off all that garish makeup. I only covered myself with fake junk because I just didn't want anyone to be attracted to me so they wouldn't hurt me like my stepfather did. But you're here now and you know where to find me now. I'm so glad to see you! You're still as beautiful as you always were."

She showed me around her apartment and Bethany came running out to hug me. I silently thanked God for sparing this little girl. Bethany grabbed my hand and pulled me toward her "own very room." It was all pink and had white furniture and toys everywhere. I felt so relieved. Whoever was responsible for this was taking very good care of them both.

She gave me a bottle of water and put some cookies out, then we nestled into her sofa to talk about what she had been through.

Reecy said, "You can stay for dinner if you like. David's mom brings so much food and her cookies are the best!"

I really wanted to accept her offer because I was very hungry from not having lunch, but I didn't want David to have to wait.

"Reecy, I can't believe how good you look." Anyone following Jesus always has that glow and I recognized it.

"I'm so glad you're here Kristi. After I told you what I was going through every day, David's mother visited me at school that same day – I mean she was there within an HOUR! I told her everything I told you. She was so sweet and understood everything! I cried and cried and she just held me. She took me to the Sanctuary hospital and then to the police. She never left my side. We filed a report and he was arrested that day and taken to jail. We then went back to our apartment and she had a talk with my mother.

My mom agreed to go into rehab and I will be able to see her in another few months. Bethany is attending school here and she loves her own room and toys. There are plenty of kids here her age to play with. David's mother comes by almost every day and she treats me like her daughter. She brings us home-cooked meals even though we really like the food in the cafeteria and can always eat there whenever we like. She buys us clothes and everything we need. Kristi, I am so happy. How did you get here?"

"Oh, David brought me and told me what happened, but he's not allowed to visit yet, so he's waiting in his Hummer while we visit."

"Wow. You two are perfect for each other. I've watched him looking at you since you started school. I'm glad you're together. He is an amazing guy."

"Oh, no, Reecy. He's just a friend. Plus I think he's dating Sasha." She would *not* tell Reecy what David had just done.

"Well, I don't know what Sasha's been saying, but there is no way he's dating her. Or anyone else for that matter. I told his mother what she did to you in the bathroom that day and all the things she was saying about David. His mother told me that David has never been interested in anyone. He's never even dated. But she did say he thought very highly of you."

Kristi remembered that he had just tried to kiss her so she didn't know how true that was.

"Well, Sasha is always talking about their dates and she has pictures of them together."

"And I'm telling you that Sasha lies – especially about David. She's been after him from day one. Everyone knows that he can't stand her and she's lying about dating him."

Kristi's mind was reeling. Could this be true? If he wasn't defiled, then that would mean . . .

She had to change this subject. "I love your apartment. Well, I suppose it's technically a condo since you have your own yard. And I love your flowers!" In reality I was feeling a tinge of jealousy, knowing how my parents were struggling and barely able to feed all of us. Could this place hold an answer to their problems? Would David's mom help them? I knew, though, they would never accept their help. They would depend on Jesus.

Reecy continued, "David's mom and I spent all day one Saturday planting the pansies. In the spring she wants to plant geraniums and impatiens. I keep them watered and now I know what weeds look like," she said laughing. She has taught me so many things and I can call her anytime with questions. I love her. And she's so good to my mom also. She's getting stronger by the day."

Then Reecy started showing all the things David's mom had given her. Such pretty clothes – nothing like what Reecy *had* been wearing. Bethany was doing her homework, but stopped to show Kristi her new dolls and clothes. Bethany was so happy and Reecy was so happy. Kristi started crying.

Reecy said, "Kristi, what's wrong?"

Reecy, I'm just so happy you're okay and Jesus is restoring you and keeping you safe and your mother is getting the medical help she needs. Can I pray for you and Bethany?"

"Please do. I love Jesus now and I love, love, LOVE being with Him and talking to Him every day. But you were right: With God, NOTHING is impossible. Thank you, Kristi, for leading me to

Jesus. And thank you for helping me escape from that monster. My life is better than I could ever imagine."

"Holy Father, thank You, THANK YOU for helping Reecy and her mom and sister. You are such a good Father. Thank You, LORD, that You let me find her again. And what a beautiful sister in Christ I have now. God, please bless her and Bethany and her mom, protect them and help them in anything they do. And I plead the precious Blood of Jesus over them. Thank You Father."

* * * * * *

David looked down at the journal peeking out of her bag. He just wanted to read one page. Then he would know if she talked to Jesus like he did. He imagined her to be so wise and mature, but was she really? One page in that journal would tell him everything he needed to know. After all, he WAS involved in all aspects of covert military operations. He could use any tactic in order to get information. Suddenly, he started getting checks in his spirit. This was wrong. These thoughts were wrong. I wouldn't want her reading *my* journal. Not yet anyway.

"Father, please forgive me. I will trust YOU, Holy Father."

He would not read that journal; he would trust God. Instead he pulled out his journal and retrieved the Christmas card. He would give it to her when she returned.

She had been there about an hour and it was getting dark and tomorrow was a school day. She hugged Reecy and Bethany and promised to come back soon. Reecy promised to get her name on the list for visitation, although this place was too far for her to walk and she would NOT ask David to take her.

Heading toward the Hummer, Kristi looked up to make sure he was still there and her heart fluttered when she saw him. He was standing next to her door waiting like he said he would. He looked so strong and handsome, but she quickly banished the thought. Why does he have this effect on me? *Lord, please help me with these temptations. My thoughts of him are not pure.*

He didn't say a word. He picked her up and put her in the passenger seat. He reached up and fastened her seat belt. When he touched her arm he saw where bruises were forming. He felt such remorse. How could he have done this to her?

Before they drove off, he handed her the card. "Please read this before you judge me too harshly."

She looked at it briefly, but she was filled with gratitude for helping Reecy. She said, "David, please forgive me for not trusting you. It's incredible what you and your parents have done to help Reecy and her mom and sister."

He sat there stunned and couldn't find the words to say to her. *She* was asking his forgiveness when he had hurt her so much worse.

"Kristi, the card explains everything and the whole time I've been gone, I didn't realize you hadn't gotten it. You don't have anything to apologize for. It was my oversight."

"I'm just so thankful she's okay. David, I was so worried. For two months I've carried this burden. I thought I had caused her great harm. I prayed continually for her and her mother and sister. I just wish I had known what your mom had done."

Then she changed the subject and started talking excitedly about everything (except the Sasha part) she and Reecy had talked about. About how different – and pretty – Reecy looked. How happy she and Bethany were. That her mother was responding so well to rehab. This visit had made Kristi happy and David was pleased. His Kristi was back. She kept laughing and talking and was bubbling with the good news after her visit. What a difference from the intense silence on the way over. He loved to see her this animated, talkative and happy. He wanted to be the reason she was happy and he would do everything in his power to make that happen. *Thank You, LORD!*

"Kristi, let me know anytime you want to visit. I will take you and wait for you, but maybe by then, I can visit as well."

She lowered her head with no response. He kept praying silently. Driving through town, he pulled up in front of his favorite Italian restaurant.

"Why are we stopping?"

"Let's get some dinner."

"Oh, I don't have the money for a place like this." In fact, she didn't have any money at all.

"Kristi, you don't ever have to pay if I ask you to dinner." He had to tell her what God had shown him about joining her mission. This would be perfect.

He helped her down again and she let him hold her hand as they walked into Little Italy. This was enough for him now. The soft Italian music played in the background and Kristi was taking in the Italian décor. She had never been to such a fancy restaurant. Mama Sophia hugged him when he came in and then hugged Kristi. She took them to a secluded table in the back with candles on the table that cast a golden glow.

When David was in the bathroom, Sophia, putting down water glasses, said, "Well, you must be very special because he's never brought a date here before."

Kristi blushed, but was pleased with the remark. She heard Frank Sinatra singing in the background, "Softly, I will leave you softly . . ." Such a sad sounding song, but she was thinking of what Reecy had said about Sasha. Could it be true? How could she find out?

Reading the menu, she all but gasped at the prices. She couldn't let David spend this kind of money, so she ordered a small salad and a water with lemon.

David said, "No, I want you to taste all this wonderful food. This is the best Italian food in the county. Miss Sophia, bring her a sampler and I'll have your famous Lasagna."

As they talked, he tried to find a segue into what God had told him about Kristi, but there just didn't seem to be an appropriate moment. He knew God would lead him, though, when the time was right.

When their food arrived, Kristi couldn't believe the portions. The sampler had lasagna, chicken marsala and chicken alfredo. She felt guilty eating any of it because she knew her parents probably only had chicken soup made from bouillon and frozen veggies. She suddenly felt sad for her parents. What would happen to them when she went to Africa? They couldn't survive.

David noticed the change in her demeanor, and said, "Kristi, what is it?"

She didn't want to tell him what she was really thinking, so she said, "I've just never been to such a nice restaurant."

He looked at her and thought, "Stay with me and I'll give you the best of everything," but instead said, "I'm glad you like it. I want to show you so many things."

She gave him a confused look and continued eating, but her mood was very different than a few hours ago. She only ate her salad and a few bites of the lasagna, hoping she could box the remainder for her parents to eat tomorrow.

When they were about to leave, Kristi asked for a go box and Sophia brought over two big bags. David took them and took Kristi's hand. Talking on the way to her house was relaxed and normal without any of the earlier anguish. He kept the conversation light and positive. He kept silently praying that God would show Kristi what He had shown him. When they arrived, he walked her to the door with the bags in tow.

Pointing to the bags Kristi said, “What is this?” There was such a gentleness and innocence when she looked at me.

“I just want your parents to experience the food at this restaurant. They will love it. The lasagna will be even better tomorrow.”

It touched her heart that he would think of them and she was filled with emotion. Tears filled her eyes, so she kept avoiding looking at him so he wouldn’t see them. He had no way of knowing their fridge was almost empty. Was God using David to supernaturally provide for them like He had used so many others to provide for them in Africa? But two big bags would help them so much and they looked so heavy. The lasagna had been so filling and should last days. *Thank You, Lord*, she silently prayed, *for blessing us.*

Her heart was filled with regret for the angry way she had confronted him. In spite of her tears, she looked into his eyes and said, “David, please forgive me for grabbing your sleeve. I had no right. I don’t know what made me do it.”

He couldn’t believe it. He had hurt her far worse than her grabbing his sleeve, yet SHE was asking forgiveness and crying about it. She lived more like Jesus than anyone he had ever met. *“God, THANK YOU!”*

“Kristi, I should be asking YOUR forgiveness. I’ve never hurt anyone like that in my life – unless they deserved it and you certainly didn’t deserve it. I don’t know what came over me. Kristi, you are so special to me. You had every right to question me about Reecy, and I should have had better control of my anger. Please forgive ME!”

"You didn't hurt me, David. I am very strong. God has blessed me with strength. Of course I forgive you."

He looked deeply into her eyes; he wanted to kiss her, but he knew she wouldn't let him. They both had school tomorrow, so he took her hand. "Good night, Kristi. I'll see you tomorrow." He brought her hand to his lips and kissed it. Her heart was racing. She knew she needed to pray about all this.

Thoroughly confused, she looked at him, remembering what Reecy had said about Sasha telling lies. Her mind racing with so many thoughts, she turned and went into the house. She would ask her momma about all of this. She knew a lot more about dating than Kristi did.

He jumped back into his truck, feeling a little better but still unsure about her feelings. Then he noticed that she had left the card. It didn't mean anything to her, yet he was saving ALL her notes to him. *"God, I know You can't make her love me, but I need Your help with this. Please help me, Lord, if this is Your Will."*

11 MARCH

Since he was still in the labs, he didn't see her again the next day. On the days he did not see her, he sank into a funk. He just drove home, threw the cards on the island and went upstairs to pray. There were so many things he didn't understand. But deep down he knew that God would lead him and He would show her His Will if he kept praying for it. *How can two walk together except they be agreed?*

She was in History, when the teacher handed her a note to immediately report to the nurse's station. Confused, she picked up her books and made her way to the station. She looked at the nameplate that read "Janet Spinner, LPN" and lightly knocked.

"Come in."

As she went in, she saw Bryan passing by and giving her a strange look as she knocked on the door. Now she was really embarrassed. He must think I'm a hypochondriac or something.

"Hi, I'm Kristi Day. Did you want to see me?"

Ms. Spinner looked her up and down. With more of a command than a request, she said "Can you please put your books on the table and have a seat?"

Kristi's heart was racing. What is this?

Sitting across from her desk, Ms. Spinner continued. "Someone has reported that there are bruises on your arm and it was suggested that your parents are physically and emotionally abusive to you."

That morning episode came flooding back. Sasha had accosted her at her locker and started making comments about her "American Gothic" inspired attire. Kristi ignored her and gathered her books so she could leave as soon as possible. Suddenly Sasha almost screamed. "What happened to your arm?"

Looking down, Kristi realized how ugly the bruises looked. Quickly rolling down her sleeve, she all but ran from Sasha, but not before she heard Sasha threaten to report it. Now she knew what Sasha had done.

"No, you don't understand, Ms. Spinner. My parents would never do something like this. These were caused by something I did. Please don't think this is in any way caused by my parents. I have the best parents in the world."

Seeming to enjoy every minute of her discomfort, Ms. Spinner said, "Can you please show me your arms?"

Not waiting for an answer, she walked over to Kristi and started rolling up the sleeves of Kristi's threadbare blouse, all the while explaining, "Yes, I hear that a lot and when I do, I become even more concerned because that kind of statement always comes from the most abused children. Children are always covering for these parents because the parents threaten them."

Her right arm was bruised from the wrist and halfway up to the elbow. To Kristi's horror, the ugly purple bruising was all the evidence Nurse Spinner needed to open a case against her parents. She could tell Ms. Spinner the truth, but then David would be in trouble. *"God please help me. Show me what to do."*

Ms. Spinner was already filling out forms – presumably to report this to Child Protective Services.

Her heart was racing. How could she explain the bruises? "Please Ms. Skinner, it's nothing. It was my fault. My parents don't even know I have these bruises."

"So they hit you and don't know about the bruising they leave?"

"No, I didn't mean it that way. My parents would never hurt me."

"Then how did you get the bruises?"

She couldn't tell her what really happened. That would get David into trouble and she would not do that to David. He had been so good to her. *"God, please help me."*

Ms. Spinner became more and more agitated. "If you don't tell me the truth RIGHT NOW, I will fill in what I KNOW to be the truth, because I KNOW your parents did this. Then, I will call the police and have your parents arrested."

By this time Kristi was crying and silently praying. *"God, please I need You. Please help me."*

* * * * * * *

David was late for school and couldn't get the preferred parking spot, but was able to get to class before the bell rang. In the middle of class, Bryan burst through the door of David's class. Ignoring the teacher's protestations, Bryan ran to David's desk and whispered something to him. David turned white and, leaving his books on his desk, ran out the door with Bryan. He ran straight to the Nurse's office. As he was about to burst through the door, he heard in his spirit, *"Video this."* He was so upset, but he KNEW where that thought originated.

Within seconds, the video was rolling and he placed the camera in the shirt pocket that had served so well in the past. Those few seconds gave him the impetus to get calmer so he could control the situation – not vice versa. David burst through the door to find Nurse Spinner holding Kristi's bruised arm, with Kristi crying. Anger flew through him because he knew Nurse Spinner used any excuse to target well-meaning parents by the most flimsy reasons. She had been the cause of many families' heartaches in dealing with Child Protective Services without solid evidence of abuse. Her Gestapo tactics were legendary and David had already been compiling evidence from other episodes to get her fired. He should have exposed this woman long ago and now he was having to deal with her personally. He knew this would get ugly.

Ms. Spinner turned on David with a vengeance not befitting a health care professional. "What are you doing in this office? GET OUT you entitled ASS!"

Very calmly (and playing to the video), David said, "Please Ms. Spinner. I don't know what Kristi's told you, but I created those bruises on Kristi's arm."

Her eyes narrowed and she moved in closer. She eyed him up and down and said, "I know who you are. You think you're hot shit in this school because your parents are loaded and think they control this town. Well, let me tell you something. This is MY department and your father can't TOUCH me. I've heard that you might be the one responsible for so much going on in this school, but you're not going to do anything about this situation. I'm going to get her parents arrested for child abuse and you or your stupid parents won't be able to do a thing about it."

Not saying a word to Ms. Spinner, he held out his hand and said, "Come on Kristi, we getting out of here. This woman is unhinged."

Kristi jumped up, grabbed her bag and held his hand. He started backing out with Kristi behind him. Ms. Spinner lunged him, clawing and scratching. With one free hand, he blocked her punches, but then decided the best thing to do would be to let her hit him. So he dropped his defense and she hit him hard across the face.

A smile broke through on David as he looked at her. He knew the camera wasn't recording HIS face. Her countenance fell and she knew what she had done. Then a new strength came over her. She said, "If you tell anyone about this, you will regret it. Do you understand me? Don't underestimate me, boy. I have connections." But she was still shaking. She knew she had just attacked the very person who COULD do something about her abusive behavior.

With Kristi still safely behind him, he looked at her with a smug grin almost and said "Have a nice day Ms. Spinner," and headed backwards through the door.

He went directly to Principal O'Reilly's office (with Kristi in tow) and played the video.

He held her hand as he walked her to class. How brave she had been in the face of such insanity. She turned to him and said, "David, I just want you to know that I didn't tell her how I got the bruises."

He still felt so bad about what he had done to her. It was like someone gut-punched him. He looked at her and said, "I know you didn't, Kristi. If you had, she wouldn't have wanted me to leave and would have tried everything in her power to have me investigated. Just pray for her."

He was so overwhelmed because she had shown loyalty to him (or, more likely, their friendship) when it would have been easier for her to just tell the truth. But she valued their friendship more than her own security. His heart overflowed with love for her. She would be one of those who would choose beheading rather than deny her Savior.

She looked deeply into his eyes, still trying to figure him out – why was he looking at her like that? Was he a sold out Christian to Jesus or a surface Christian with one foot in the world and one foot in religion? She liked him so much. Why had he allowed himself to be so taken in by the world? Her heart was sad for him (and maybe a little for herself). Since she could never prove that he wasn't defiled, she could NOT let herself become attached to him. She firmly believed Reecy didn't have all the facts. She decided to avoid contact with him at all cost. She desperately needed to get back to Africa and nothing, especially play-church Christians, would stop her.

He wanted so much to know her thoughts. He wouldn't have liked them though. She was still lamenting his defilement. She thanked him (not making the eye contact that he had come to live for) and went into class.

The next day everyone was talking about the pretty new nurse for the school.

12 MARCH: WEEK 4

Some time had gone by without seeing him, but thoughts of him constantly invaded her mind. Since she was taking accelerated classes, she no longer saw him in Speech Class. She wasn't being bullied now that he was back – just a few ignorable comments. She noticed that Stephen was no longer following her, and she now felt vulnerable again not having Stephen or David around to run interference for her. Her mind, though, was constantly playing the memories of the times she and David had shared. She missed him.

Not able to sleep as well, she had gotten up late and almost missed the bus. They even had to forgo their prayers and devotion this morning. She had also forgotten to bring her water, and had not eaten anything the previous day because she had forgotten her lunch money. Actually her mother had "forgotten" to give it to her again. She knew her dad's hours had been cut at Value Mart because management had caught him witnessing to another employee. Value Mart rarely fired anyone, they just cut their hours so much that they left on their own. How long would they be able to pay the rent? She didn't want to burden them about her lunch money, but she was hungry and thirsty. The food from the Italian restaurant had lasted them a week, but now the fridge was as bare as before. *"God, please help us."*

As she was making her way to class, she looked down at a scuffed up ticket. To her surprise she discovered it was an unpunched lunch ticket. Since it was untraceable, this meant she could eat lunch that day. *"Thank You JESUS!"* But she still needed some water. She was so thirsty. She spotted the water fountain a short distance away, but saw Zach, Larry and Dean lurking over it. Every time she saw Zach now, he gave her piercing evil looks. She knew he was plotting some kind of revenge against her and Stephen and David were nowhere around. She could only pray that Zach hadn't noticed their absence. She couldn't risk being accosted at the fountain, so she headed to class without the much-needed water.

Finally, she walked into the lunchroom, went through the line with her chicken and vegetable meal and the precious water. When she was praying over her food, she felt someone sit down across from her. When she opened her eyes, her heart sank. It was Zach, Larry and Dean. Her fears were manifesting before her eyes. Stephen rarely ate in the lunchroom and she hadn't seen David since last week. Zach started tormenting her with disgusting sexual remarks while Larry and Dean sat silent, but obviously enjoying his remarks and her discomfort. When he got no response, he took the salt and ketchup and poured it over her food. He poured pepper in her water and kept taunting her. She knew she had to leave, but her book bag was almost on his side of the table and she couldn't risk retrieving it. He would have grabbed it if he knew she wanted it, so she just sat there. *"Lord,"* she prayed silently, *"please help me . . . again."*

Suddenly the entire lunchroom went completely quiet. She looked up to see everyone looking at someone behind her. She could feel him. She knew David or Stephen was behind her and was about to do something. She looked up at Zach whose face went pale. He pushed his chair back with false bravado and said, "Well, it was a great lunch, wasn't it Kristi?" He then turned and left quickly. Eventually the lunchroom returned to normal, so she assumed David or Stephen had left. Her heart was pounding and her head was spinning. She needed water.

Bryan motioned David over to his table just behind Kristi's table. Bryan had already eaten, but David pulled out his Chick-fil-A bag. Bryan said, "Why don't you ask Kristi to join us. Those guys ruined her food and she hasn't had anything." David looked over and saw what they had done. The pigs. He stood up to go ask her, and about the same time, she stood up to leave. She started to reach for her bag, when she felt the blackness flood over her. As her knees began to buckle, she knew she was fainting. *"Jesus!"*

As he saw her falling, he rushed to catch her before she hit the floor. He scooped her up and instructed Bryan to grab the book bags – his and Kristi's. Byran also grabbed David's food and ran ahead to man the doors. Turning right to the Nurse's station, David said, "No, go to Sampson. I have all my paramedic supplies there." Bryan ran to the large double doors and held them open. He made his way to the Hummer and Bryan was already there with the back seat door opened. David stepped up and laid her in the back seat. He propped her up on a pillow and opened the medic bag. He pulled out a stethoscope, put on gloves and pulled out an ammonia ampule. He unbuttoned her top buttons and listened to her heart. Very strong, so the ammonia would not have an adverse effect. He lowered the stethoscope behind his ears, but kept the diaphragm on her wrist to monitor her heart rate. Bryan was opening the other door for air circulation. David said, "Bryan, grab some water and Gatorade. And some straws."

He broke open the ampule. She turned quickly away from the smell and looked around until she was looking into his eyes. His heart melted, but he didn't say a word.

"What happened?"

Bryan said, "You fainted Kristi."

She closed her eyes. She was so embarrassed. "What is happening NOW? I have got to get out of this school."

David was afraid she meant it.

"Did I hit my head?"

Bryan said, "No, David caught you before you hit the floor."

She looked at David and he was looking at her. He wanted to kiss her, but he was in full capacity as a paramedic – and not a civilian. He could lose his license.

"I forgot my water . . . and I haven't eaten in two days."

She didn't mean to say that; she didn't want them to think that she was too poor to eat and pity her. "I've just been so busy and . . . and."

"Yes," David said, "we have to get your electrolytes back in balance."

They heard the bell ring and Bryan said, "Well, I've got to get to class." He primarily wanted them to be alone.

Kristi sat up and moved to go and said, "I've got to get to class too."

David said, "Not on my watch. We've got to get you back to normal first."

"But what about your class?"

There it was again – Kristi more concerned about others than her own welfare.

As he put the straw of the water to her lips, he said "Kristi, there is no class as important as what we're both doing right now."

She hungrily drank the water. "That is so good," she said. She drank and drank. Finally she looked up at him.

He still had the stethoscope on her wrist.

She had missed him so much and now he was right here with her.

Still looking at him, she said, "David, why are you so good to me?"

The question shocked him. He stammered and said, "Well . . . you . . . you're just very easy to be good to."

She looked away. He knew it was a stupid answer and he could kick himself for being so disingenuous. Tell her the truth man!

She looked back at him again – almost demanding a truthful answer, "Why do you keep helping me?"

He became unglued inside. Should I give her another fake answer or do I risk losing her by telling her my true feelings? *Lord, please help me with this.* He then knew what Jesus would do.

She was still looking at him. . .. Time stopped.

"Because I love you."

He could hear his heart beating through the stethoscope. It was so loud he was afraid she would hear it also. Then he realized he still had the stethoscope on her wrist and was hearing HER heartbeat. She was feeling the same emotion, but to look at her, she was the epitome of calm and composure. Not one evidence of her emotions. If she had this much control on showing her true feelings, how could I know if she was feeling the same love for me?

She whispered a weak, "Oh," and just kept looking into his eyes. What was she thinking? *Lord, please guide me. I need Your help, Lord.*

He wanted to kiss her now more than ever. It took every ounce of inner strength to hold back.

Finally, he knew she needed to eat (and to take his mind off of an almost uncontrollable urge to take her in his arms), he said, "Are you hungry?"

Still looking at him, she nodded yes.

He removed the stethoscope, pulled off his gloves and took out the CFA bag. He was officially off duty as a paramedic and could get back to being David Everett, unapologetic lover of Kristi Day! He gave her a sandwich and they both enjoyed lunch. He did not want this time to end. He fed her some of his super salad and they both shared an intimate time with this meal. Something, though, had definitely shifted in the atmosphere and this time they both felt it.

After about 30 minutes, Kristi said, "David, I need to get back to class. I'm okay now."

He said, "Kristi, I think you should wait. Your electrolytes were really out of whack."

"No," she said. "I'm okay now, really."

He put all of his medical supplies back in the bag and told her to wait.

He went around to the other side and helped her out. When she stood up, she faltered, but he held onto her.

He held her closer than he normally would in this situation, but he was a civilian now. He said "I wish I had made you wait longer."

Holding onto him, she said, "I wish I had listened to you."

Love flooded through him and reminded him of the many times he had felt the presence of God. He made up his mind right there. He opened the front seat passenger door and lifted her up. "You're not going back to class today. I'm taking you home."

Because she was still feeling weak, she did not fight him on this.

Since she didn't want to get home too early (her mother would have been worried if she found out Kristi had fainted), he drove to the park just around the corner from her house. He was going to tell her today!

They drove around and found a shady, secluded spot looking out over the lake. People were walking dogs and playing Frisbee golf. They filled the time with gentle conversation.

A gentle breeze blew through the open windows and the smell of blooming wisteria wafted in. He was in heaven. "*God*," he prayed silently, *"please help me find the right words. Please Lord, show her what You've shown me."*

Finally, he turned towards her. "Kristi, I know I probably freaked you out when I said I love you, but I have never said those words to any girl. I also want to tell you about something the Lord has shown me."

She turned away from him and remembering all of the painful Sasha conversations, she said, "Please, David. I really don't want to talk about this right now. My head is still spinning and I can't think logically. Plus, I have to pray about this."

"I know, Kristi, but this is important. I just . . .

"But, David, I don't think we're of one accord. Something doesn't seem right. There are too many things that don't make sense to me. Things I've heard from others. I need to talk to my momma. I need to pray with her."

"Well, will you let me take you to dinner on Friday so we can talk?"

Kristi, remembering her plans for Africa and all the pictures Sasha had talked about and has shown others, said, "David, I just don't think it's a good idea. Plus, I'll be leaving for Africa soon. You just need to forget about me."

13 APRIL

A blackness surrounded David and there was nothing he could do about it. He started Samson and drove her home in silence. When he lifted her out, she wouldn't even look at him and just offered a weak, "Thank you for helping me," and ran into the house.

The blackness continued. He was sinking into a depression he'd never known and couldn't even muster the faith to ask God to help him. It seemed a black fog was overtaking his thoughts and feelings and he couldn't push back the fog. He knew it was a spiritual attack, but he was too dragged down and broken hearted to do anything about it. He would ask his father to cast it out. A few weeks before on the island, he had felt like one of the strongest men in the world. Now he felt like the weakest.

The next day and for the first time in two years, he called out sick from school. His mother knocked on his door several times, but he asked her quietly to just let him be alone. She respected his request. She and Helga prayed fervently throughout the day for David, and Helga baked his favorite Oatmeal cookies. His mother fixed a tray for him and put it outside his door. She heard him praying in his closet. She had never seen him like this – ever, and she knew this had to do with Kristi.

Later she saw him sitting in a lounge chair overlooking the pool. She saw he was lost in thought.

She sat down a glass of iced tea on the table next to him. Then she sat down in the chair beside his.

"David, tell me about Kristi."

David felt relief flood him because he wanted to talk about her more than anything. His mother had known about his feelings all along.

"Mom, she's just so different from anyone I've ever met. When I first met her, I thought she was shy and had low self esteem. People bullied her and she never defended herself, so I wrote her off as a coward and perpetual victim. Mom, I was so wrong about her. She's one of the strongest girls I've ever met and she has such compassion for people – especially for the bullies. The bullies?!? In fact, the first time I had any interaction with her, Sasha had sneaked up behind her and pushed her down the stairs. I dived sideways and caught her. I knew God had arranged that meeting for us. Then she said she tripped instead of blaming Sasha. She KNEW Sasha had pushed her, but she didn't want ME to feel anger at Sasha. Can you believe that? Whenever she was being bullied, she just waited patiently until they got tired of it. She wasn't offended at all. Mom, she's just so different and so much more mature than her age. She puts me to shame in a lot of ways – especially the way she encourages me to pray for people who try to hurt us. She truly acts more like Jesus than anyone I know."

"I know son. Reecy told me that Sasha AND Reecy had said such vile things to Kristi, but she never seemed offended. Reecy told me she even slapped Kristi once, but Kristi cared more for what Reecy was going through than she did with being slapped. Reecy said she tried everything to get Kristi to leave her alone, but Kristi wouldn't. She really cared about Reecy. And because of that, Reecy is safe now – because of Kristi acting like Jesus would have acted – being the apostle Jesus commanded us to be. You're right, she is very special."

David turned to his mother, "Mom, I KNOW God is trying to put us together, but she doesn't want me and I don't know why. I know you can't make someone love you, but I've only been nice to her and supportive. She told me last night that she's going to Africa and that I should forget about her. So apparently she doesn't want me to help her in Africa. She even left the Christmas card in my truck – it meant so little to her. Mom, what can I do?"

"David, I really don't know. I think we need to pray about this. Just ask our Father what His Will is. He will guide you. Just remember, whatever you do, we love you and we will support any decision you make. I love you."

"I love you, mom."

Mrs. Everett mourned for her son. She wished she had the power to take away his pain. Why wouldn't Kristi have anything to do with him? He was incredibly handsome, smart, loved Jesus – everything Kristi *should* want in someone. It must be something else – or someone else. Was her heart given to another? She remembered the Jewish axiom: A mother is only as happy as her saddest child. Unfortunately, she now knew the magnitude of the saying. *"God, please give him Your Peace."* She and Helga continued to pray for David and Kristi. Deep down she also knew that Kristi was the one God had chosen for David. Somehow this knowledge gave her great peace.

After she left, he just started talking to God. *"Lord, please show me what I've done to attract these attacks. Please forgive me for anything I've done or caused someone hurt. God, I love her and I want her in my life. I know You have put us together, but I need for You to show her as well. I thank You, Lord, that You watch over Your Word to perform it. Amen."*

That night he dreamed of her. They were walking in the same park he had left earlier. She was holding his hand. They were both laughing and felt right being together. Then white balloons began to fall from the sky. Kristi let go of his hand and started chasing the balloons. The balloons became so thick he kept losing sight of her. Finally he cried, "Kristi, don't leave me!" He sat up in bed with his mother shaking him awake.

"David, you were having a nightmare."

He burrowed his head in her arms. "Mom, what am I going to do? I love her and I know God has led me to her, but she won't have anything to do with me. She doesn't want me like I want her. Mom, what can I do?"

She said, "You're going to trust the Lord and you're going to pray for His Will. He will never leave you nor forsake you."

"Holy Father, in the name of Jesus, please help David with this situation. You said in Your Word 'Trust in the Lord with all your heart, and lean not on your own understanding. In all your ways acknowledge Him, and He will direct your paths.' Thank You Lord for leading David out of this dark time."

She held David until he fell back to sleep. She wished she could help David with this hurt, but he wasn't a little boy anymore, but that didn't stop her from holding him and worrying about him. He had grown into a big, strong, confidant man and she was proud of his accomplishments, but she was powerless in this situation. All she could do was pray. *"Father, please open Kristi's eyes to Your Will in this – IF this is Your Will that they find each other."*

* * * * * * *

After David had taken her home, she told her mother about the conflicting feelings she was having for David. She said, "Momma, I need you to pray for me. David wants to date me, but I think he's been with someone else and maybe *still* seeing her. He says he hasn't dated her or anyone, but this girl says they *are* dating but he doesn't want others to know. But she's constantly showing her friends pictures of them together and telling them about their dates. Momma, I really like him. He's so nice to me and he has such a compassionate heart, and he loves Jesus and talks to Him like we do. He's done so much to help me. He's so good to me and I *really* like him, but I don't want him if he's a liar. What should I do momma?"

"Kristi, have *you* prayed about this?"

"Yes, momma, but I'm not getting any answers. I just know I really like being with him. He appears so gentle and kind, but I don't know if it's just an act and he's just playing with me."

"Why haven't you told me about your feelings for him before?"

"I don't know, momma. I just like him so much and I know he likes me because he's always looking at me. I'm just so shy around him. But it's what Sasha is always saying that is so confusing."

"Well, Kristi, sometimes people don't always tell the truth. Have you seen them together?"

"Well, no, but sometimes she talks to him at our lockers and in class."

"So, you've never seen them holding hands or affectionate towards each other?"

"Well . . . no, momma, but she talks about their dates and says she has pictures. Intimate pictures. Oh, but whenever she tries to talk to him, he looks at her like he's annoyed and gets away from her quickly."

Kristi's mom smiled and said, "Well, that doesn't seem to me like they're dating. Doesn't even sound like he likes her."

"She says he only acts that way because he's the most popular boy in school and he doesn't want anyone to know they're dating."

"Kristi, does he hold your hand?"

Kristi looked down thinking. "Yes, momma. He does."

"Does he do it in the open or does he try to hide it from others?"

"In the open."

"Does he go out of his way to talk to you?"

"Yes."

"Does he talk to other girls like he talks to you?"

"No, momma. Not that I've seen. I mean, he's nice to everyone."

Then she realized that he was *not* nice to Sasha. "Everyone . . . everyone EXCEPT SASHA! Momma, he doesn't like her at all!"

"Well, seems to me that you've got your answer. YOU'RE the one he likes. Kristi, just because you don't tell lies doesn't mean other people don't. Even if someone is very beautiful, if he doesn't respect her, then they don't have a relationship. Let's see what the Lord has to say about this." She took Kristi's hand and they prayed protection, favor and blessings over Kristi. She prayed that God would reveal HIS WILL and what Kristi should do in this matter. She thanked the Lord and prayed the Aaronic blessing over her beautiful daughter. The daughter with whom the Lord had blessed them. She would add Kristi and David to her prayers.

That night, Kristi dreamed that she was in heaven walking down a beautiful lane. She stopped by a grove of lush rose bushes and waited. The glorious smell of roses swirled around her and permeated her skin. She kept waiting – for what she didn't know. Then she saw Jesus walking towards her. He smiled at her. He had someone by the hand, but she couldn't see who it was. As Jesus neared her, she was about to drop to her knees before Him, but He held out His hand to her instead, which she eagerly took. They all walked together for a while. Then they came to a big, flat rock. Jesus helped the other person to the rock and then helped Kristi up. The rock felt warm on her feet. She then turned to look at the person next to her and looked right into David's eyes. He put his arm around her and she put her head on his shoulder. A sweet peace came over her and she woke with a start. She knew then she had the answer.

"Oh, thank You LORD for showing me this dream. I KNOW what You want now and I know that David is the man You have promised me. THANK YOU!"

She was so excited to get to school. She tried to look especially nice and tied a pink ribbon in her hair. She knew it was a dated look, but it was all she had. Her shoes looked so shabby, so she tried to clean them as best she could. Maybe he wouldn't notice. For the first time, she was almost ashamed of her clothes. David always dressed well. He looked so neat and put together and she looked so shabby next to him.

"Father, please forgive me for feeling sorry for myself. You've been so good to us. How could I even feel sorry for myself? You said that ALL things work together for good to those who love You and I DO love You Lord. Thank You for blessing me in so many ways."

At school, she looked for David all day so she could apologize and tell him about her dream. She asked Bryan where he was, and Bryan said he had called out sick. He showed her how to look up school attendance on the phone. But since she didn't own a phone or a computer, it was a moot point.

She hoped he was okay and that he would get over the sickness quickly. She thought about every time he had been nice to her; every time he had come to her defense; every time she had looked into his eyes. Every time that had happened, she felt like he was trying to tell her he loved her. Was that her imagination? Since her dream, she wanted to be with him now more than ever. She wanted to talk to him. She wanted to share her feelings. And, yes, she had to know if he had been with Sasha. *"God, please heal him quickly. Thank You Jesus."*

Even if he had been with Sasha, she didn't believe they were together now – regardless of what she said. The thought of him being with her, however, made her feel queasy. God had promised her someone undefiled, but maybe that was expecting too much in this day and age. She wished she had read the Christmas Card and she wished she had put it in her bag, but she had left it in the truck. What had he said? She would ask him tomorrow after she apologized.

The next day she was standing with Bryan, Jonny and Richie when David appeared down the hall. He was still suffering from this spiritual depression. He went to his locker, pulled out some books and started walking towards them. Then he spotted her and stopped abruptly. He looked at Richie, then at her. She looked straight at him and gave him an expectant smile. She looked so happy, but remembering her last words, he gave her an angry look, then darted down the stairwell to avoid having to talk to anyone. How could she look so happy when I'm so miserable? Is she with Richie now? *"God, help me get over her."*

Kristi was crestfallen at David's angry look and big tears came into her eyes. Why had he given her that angry look? Then she remembered her last words to him. But it had changed now. She wanted to tell him about the dream. Should I go after him? Should I just explain everything in a letter? He must hate me now. *"Lord, please help me; I've messed this up. He hates me and I can't blame him."* Kristi left hurriedly so no one would see her tears.

Bryan had witnessed the entire encounter. He had seen David's angry look at Kristi; he had seen Kristi's tears. He didn't know the details, but he did know there was a miscommunication. He would try to fix this. He could *not* let these two separate when it looked so promising after he had left them in the truck. *God, please help me with these two!*

Bryan bolted down the stairwell after David. There he was at the bottom in the corner shadows. Bryan saw that he was very agitated – almost to the point of tears.

"David, why didn't you come talk to us?"

Pacing, David said, "I . . .I just didn't feel like it."

He challenged David: "David, Are you insane?"

Surprised at Brian's chastisement, he stopped pacing and said, "What do you mean?"

"Didn't you see the way Kristi looked at you when she saw you? She was waiting for YOU, man. She was so happy and I've never seen her like that around you. And she was asking where you were yesterday and kept looking for you. She wanted to tell you something."

David's face fell. "Oh man. Bryan, what have I done now? But she turned me down when I asked her out. She told me to forget about her. I wanted to tell her what the Lord had shown me, but she didn't want to hear it. I don't know what to do."

"Well, I think something important has changed with her. She was so excited about telling you something. Something I think the Lord has revealed to *her*. I could tell she was really anxious yesterday."

"Really? Bryan, what should I do?"

"Here's what you do. Go FIND her and apologize for being a jerk and tell her what's in your heart."

"Well, I tried that already, but I'm willing to do anything."

Suddenly he had a vision. He was standing in a small living room when he heard something behind him. He turned. It was Kristi. She reached up to him and he picked her up. The vision ended. This gave him the hope he needed. *Tears last for a night, but JOY comes in the morning.* Hallelujah!

The bell rang for class, so it would have to wait. David raced down the hall to his next class, but he knew his mind would not be on the class.

14 THE ATTACK

Kristi was taking semester and final tests in the Testing Lab all week, so David wouldn't have been able to find her if he tried. The Testing Lab was on the fourth floor at the far end of the school in an almost deserted area. There were no other classes at that end of the hall. The teacher had instructed her to put her test on top of the desk when finished and the teacher left. She really liked being able to be alone to take the tests. When she finished, it was almost time for the end of school. She decided to just board the bus early so she could write in her journal.

She started down the deserted stairwell that led to an outside door on the bottom floor. As she reached the 3rd floor, she heard a noise. Before she could do anything, Zach, Larry and Dean had her surrounded. Fear flooded her in every fiber of her being. She knew she was all alone. She knew no one knew where she was; there was no one to help her. She knew that Zach was ready to take his revenge on her. How could she fight three big guys?

Instinctively, she put her bag up to her chest. This seemed to inflame Zach as he grabbed the bag and threw it to the floor. *"God, please help me."* She was so scared and trembling. Zach told the others to guard the doors and not let anyone in the stairwell. He slammed her up against the wall and started pawing her. She tried to pull away, but he caught her threadbare blouse and tore it almost off. *"God, please help me."*

"Your God's not going to be able to help you now, you bitch. You think that boyfriend of yours can find you over here? He doesn't even know where you are. So which boyfriend are you givin' it to this week? David or Stephen? You think you're so much better than we are with your fake religion. Where's your God now? Before I finish with you, you'll look worse than I did after Stephen jumped me. Better yet, I have something else in mind for you, bitch!"

He slapped her hard. She went down on one knee and felt blood trickle from her mouth. He took advantage of her crippled position and pushed her to the floor, dragging her behind the stairs. She was trying to fight as much as possible. He was so strong. *"GOD HELP ME!"*

* * * * * * *

Minutes earlier in class, something jerked David out of his desk. He knew Kristi was in trouble. He started praying. He jumped up, ran out of class and ran to the front of the building. He knew exactly where Kristi was and he knew the quickest way to get there. He ran across the front of the school, up the side stairs to the third floor and ran to the stairwell door at the end. He knew someone was blocking that door, so he used all his strength to burst through. This sent Larry headfirst down the stairs. Dean tried to run down the stairs, but not before David kicked him in the rear, sending him to join Larry. Then he saw Zach on top of Kristi. With

Herculean strength from the over abundance of adrenalin and unbridled anger at what he was trying to do, he picked up Zach, lifting him almost over his head. He looked down to the bottom floor and could have easily thrown him there – possibly killing him. But instead, he threw him over the stairs onto the next landing. He heard something break on Zach, but he didn't care. Kristi was crouched in the corner crying. He saw that her blouse had been torn off, but she was covered with a torn slip. He saw the blood around her mouth. He took off his shirt and put it around her. He sat down on the dirty floor and pulled her to him. She was trembling so hard.

He held her as she cried and stammered, "I tr.. tr- tried to fight him. I . . .I tried."

David soothed her, "Kristi you couldn't fight those cowards. Those are three big guys. You're not meant to be able to fight them. But you're safe now and I will never let anyone hurt you again. You're with me now; you're safe." He held her tightly and he felt her tears and cradled her trembling body. He just held her – just like he'd been taught.

She was clutching his t-shirt. "Why do they hate me so much?" she stammered.

He pulled her closer. "Kristi, they really hate themselves. Your goodness highlights the darkness of their hearts. Remember, Jesus said 'They hated Me and they will hate you also.' So consider it all joy when people revile you."

She pulled in closer to him. The love he felt for her was overwhelming

"Father, in the name of Jesus, I bind any demonic spirit trying to come against Kristi. I rebuke the spirit of lust; I rebuke the spirit of fear; and I cast all spirits that have tried to come upon Kristi from this experience to the feet of Jesus for Him to judge. Father, I

ask that You loose Your spirit of peace. Let her rest in Your Holy Arms, Father and I plead the precious Blood of Jesus over her."

He held her for a very long time quoting every comforting scripture he could think of. When he looked down, he knew she was already asleep. He was glad. He would stay there all night if necessary, but he pulled out his phone and texted the principal to wait for him until he got there. After a few hours, he could hear that most had left and the school was very quiet. She woke up then and asked him to take her home. He said, "Kristi, we have to report this. Those guys need to be expelled."

"Oh, I don't want to do that. They need to graduate, and they didn't hurt me really."

I was shocked. "Are you kidding me? Kristi, these guys attacked you – they must be brought to justice. Other girls may be in danger or be harmed if they're allowed to walk. We can have righteous anger, Kristi."

She nodded in agreement. He lifted her up. "Come on. The principal is waiting for us."

In the Principal's office, David began explaining what he found when he entered the stairwell while Kristi seemed to climb into a quiet shell, wrapping David's shirt even more tightly around her. He told the whole story and insisted that Zach, Larry and Dean be expelled.

Principal O'Reilly said, "Kristi, do you need to go to the hospital?"

Not even looking up, she shook her head no.

"Kristi, what on earth were you doing in that stairwell?"

David turned on him instantly, "Wait a minute. This is not HER fault. She should be able to walk ANYWHERE in this school without being accosted."

"You're absolutely right. Kristi, I'm sorry for being so insensitive."

Principal O'Reilly said, "Well, we have to investigate this matter; unless they've made terroristic threats, we can't expel anyone without unanimous School Board approval – especially if Kristi won't file a police report."

Kristi couldn't believe how David was talking to the Principal – almost as if David were in charge. David didn't even respond to what the Principal had said. He was making a phone call. "Dad? I just caught Zach, Larry and Dean attacking Kristi. Zach was trying to rape her. I want these guys expelled. Can you call the Board and get a decision back ASAP? Yes, she's with me. No, she's okay. *Thank You, JESUS!* Thanks Dad. I love you."

He hung up and looked straight at the Principal. "Mr. O'Reilly, I know you have to follow certain procedures and I do respect that, but how would you feel if you caught someone within seconds of raping your wife?"

O'Reilly couldn't believe what he was hearing. Now he understood and this was all beginning to make sense and he was blown away. This was not just someone David was helping. The great David Everett was in LOVE with Kristi Day. But he thought about his own sweet wife and said "I would want to kill them."

"Well, I wanted to kill them too. But I didn't and you know full well I could have. I'm pretty sure Zach's arm is broken, so there may be an evidence trail from the local hospital."

Kristi was shocked at what she was hearing. First, he had talked to his dad about her as if his dad already knew about her. His dad had even asked about her condition. Then he had compared her to a wife. Added to the confusion was his comment about killing someone. Plus, he was talking to the Principal as an equal – not as a student. Then she remembered that Mr. Watkins had never returned to school after his interaction with David. And the nurse had left so suddenly. Then she remembered that Stephen had stopped following her after David's return. What in the world? Did David have that much power? She just wanted to go home and take a bath. She felt so dirty. She could smell him from his shirt and she wanted to wrap herself in that smell. That smell meant safety.

The phone rang on the Principal's desk.

"Yes, yes, thank you. Can you e-mail that to me? I'll have security get right on it. Yes, she seems to be doing better, but I think she's pretty tough. Yes, I'll take care of that too. Thank you, Richard."

David looked at him. "Okay, it's done. Kristi, you won't ever have to worry about those three again."

David shook hands with the principal, then reached out his hand to Kristi as if it was the most natural thing to do. She willingly took it. He put his arm around her as they walked out.

* * * * * * *

It was getting very late and no one had called her parents. David dialed their number and explained everything that happened. When they walked in the door, Kristi ran from David's arms into her mother's arms. They went into the back of the house, leaving David with Mr. Day. He gave more details of the attack. Mr. Day began shaking his head, tears coming into his eyes. "I think I made a mistake coming back to the U.S. This place has so much evil now. We just feel so trapped."

"Mr. Day. Please don't give up just yet. I will make a vow to you tonight. I will never let anyone hurt her. I love your daughter, Mr. Day."

Kristi's mom came back in at that point. Her face was white. "Kristi's not hurt really. Her lip will be swollen, but thank God nothing else was damaged."

David knew what she meant by that and said a silent prayer. *"Father, thank You for protecting her and saving her for me."*

"She's taking a bath, but we want to thank you, son, for saving our daughter. Kristi told me what you did. But she didn't know how you KNEW where she was. She was so far away from the other classes; she was in the Testing Labs. There was no way you could have known where she was."

"I didn't know either. I was sitting in class when I felt something – an angel maybe – jerk me out of my desk. I knew Kristi was in trouble and somehow I knew exactly where she was. I just ran as fast as I could. I can't explain it, but I've always felt a spiritual connection with Kristi."

"Well, thank you and thank GOD that He is protecting you both."

"Oh," David said remembering the dinner invitation. "My mom and dad really admire you and your mission work. In fact, she met you both when you preached at their church before they were married – and they credit you with them becoming missionaries. When they heard your testimony of being missionaries, my mom and dad knew what God wanted them to do. They became missionaries in South America for several years before coming back to the States to have my sister, Beth. She is now a missionary in South America. My parents are very anxious to meet you. Mom wants to know if you all can come to dinner week after next? A Saturday or a Sunday – whatever is best for you. There is so much my parents want to thank you for. You have no idea how your ministry has affected our ministry. In fact, we still pray for your ministry when we have our devotions every morning."

Stunned and humbled at this confession, Mr. Day said, "Okay, we'll talk it over and let you know."

Mrs. Day walked over and hugged him. "Thank you again, David. You're such a God-send."

He felt such love from this family. And he wanted them to become a part of his family. *"Thank You Jesus!"*

On the way home, David realized the funk had left. He knew God had given him this gift. He thought about that last vision. In that vision, Kristi was wearing his shirt. Were he and Kristi finally on the same page? *"Thank You JESUS!"*

* * * * * * *

She was not at school the next day, but he wasn't surprised. It was Friday and he planned to go visit her after school.

"Mom?" Can you make some dinner and stuff so I can take it to Kristi's tonight? She wasn't in school today. I just want to make sure she's okay."

His mom smiled and was grateful that her prayers about David and Kristi may have been answered. She just had a peace about it all.

His mother had really come through. There were four big shopping bags full of dinners and pies, bread, butter, even candy – nothing was left out. It was already past 7:30, but he wanted to get to the Days' before they went to bed.

He was there by 8:30 and took the bags to the door and knocked. Mr. Day answered and David gave the bags to him. "My mom made this for you. She is so sorry about what happened, and I just need to make sure she's okay."

"Son, you shouldn't be doing this. This is too much."

"Oh, but you don't understand. My mom loves to do this and does this for many people. She brings food to people for any situation and our housekeeper, Helga, is one of the best cooks around. Her meals are delicious. You'll see when you try these meals and when you come to dinner next week. Oh, and you don't have to return the casserole dishes. My mom buys them in bulk when she finds them at thrift stores. Just use them or pay it forward."

Kristi's mom came from the kitchen area while Mr. Day took the food to the refrigerator.

Mrs. Day said, "David, Kristi's still sleeping. She's been sleeping all day. I'm a little worried."

"Mrs. Day, it's good that Kristi is sleeping. She's been through some trauma and the more she sleeps, the better the recovery will be. She may need some counseling, and my parents can provide someone from the Sanctuary. That's their mission."

He further explained about the trauma/sleep training he had been through and this seemed to assuage her worry. He explained how his family had helped so many victims this way.

He had his back to her bedroom door, but heard a slight sound (or maybe just felt her spirit). He turned and saw her standing in the doorway still wearing his shirt. Their eyes locked and instinctively, she lifted her arms to him. He gently picked her up and sat down in a chair with her in his lap with her legs draped over the side. He held her tightly and the world became a blur. He was in heaven. *Thank You LORD!* SHE had lifted her arms to me. *Thank You LORD!* It was just like it was in the vision. God had given him that vision to reassure him that God had everything under control. Even so, David had felt doubt and unbelief. *"Lord, please forgive me for doubting You. Thank You Lord for this incredible blessing! My GOD. In HIM will I trust."*

Mrs. Day covered Kristi's legs with a small throw and placed a small pillow behind David's head. She went into Kristi's room and turned down the bed. She then placed a tumbler of water next to David as she cut out the lights.

Knowing this was Kristi's "David," she said "Stay as long as you like son. I've turned down her bed when you decide to leave."

With his free hand, David took Mrs. Day's hand and kissed it. "Thank you, Mrs. Day."

"Call me Ally."

When Mrs. Day entered her bedroom, she looked at her husband and said, "John, I think we've just met our future son in law."

He smiled at the thought. He knew Kristi well enough that she would not settle for just anyone, and David seemed to have all the right qualifications.

"Yes, he told me he loved her, but we still need to pray about it and see what God says," and turned out the light.

* * * * * * *

He held her until he heard the clock strike 4. He didn't want to still be there when they got up, so he carried her to bed and covered her. He leaned down, kissed her and said, "I love you Kristi" and left. In her sleepiness, she whispered, "I love you too David," but he was already gone.

15 HIT AND RUN

She was back at school on Tuesday but still in the Testing lab, but this time the teacher stayed throughout all testing. She was grateful for that. She wanted so much to talk to David and hoped she would see him before she left. There was such an energy in the air, she couldn't explain it. Things seemed to be happening so quickly. What ELSE could happen in this school?

David had missed her all week. He knew she was in the Testing Labs and would come find him when she was ready. On Thursday, he saw her heading to the bus and called to her. Before he could get to her, he saw a white Ford truck jump the curb and head straight towards her. Then Jason, riding his bicycle from the bike rack to the road, and not seeing the truck, rode right out in front of it. The truck side-swiped the bike and Jason was flung off, crashing to the sidewalk. The truck peeled off without even checking to see about the rider. David ran back to his Hummer for his med bag.

Kristi had seen Jason fall and the truck leave and had rushed over to administer first aid. She saw that he was bleeding profusely in his arm and suspected artery damage. She ripped the ruffle from around her skirt and started trying to tie a tourniquet. David arrived just in time to help her with the tourniquet. He also supported Jason's legs with his med bag. David looked at Kristi as she took control of the situation with calm efficiency. He was so proud of her. She had such inner strength and they both knew where that strength originated. *Be strong in the Lord and the power of His might.* They both started praying for Jason.

David saw they were all covered in blood, and tried to calm Jason while they waited for the ambulance. The ambulance finally arrived and took Jason to the hospital, as David and Kristi gave their reports to the police. No one had been able to get a tag number.

David grabbed Kristi's hand and his med bag as they both ran to his Hummer. He handed Kristi his cell phone. "Call your mom and tell her what's happened and that we're headed to the hospital."

They were not allowed in the family-only Critical Care waiting room, so they found a seldom-used smaller room around the corner from CCU. Since they were alone in the waiting room, they both knelt down and held hands to pray for Jason.

They prayed for Jason, his parents and prayed the driver of the truck would do the right thing and turn himself in. David looked over at Kristi praying. *"God, thank You that you've allowed me this time with her. Please don't let me screw it up."*

Kristi settled on the small sofa and looked up to David. "What else can we do for them?"

David said, "We can't do much but wait for word of his condition. Here's my phone. Call you mom and tell her the status."

She took the phone about the time he stood up and said, "Wait here; I'm going to Samson to get a change of clothes."

Kristi looked down at her torn skirt and blood-covered blouse. Now she was down to ONE outfit and she knew her parents didn't have the money to buy her anything new. Ordinarily she wouldn't care, but for some reason, she did care what David thought and didn't want him seeing her looking so shabby, but there was little she could do about it. For a split second, she almost began to feel sorry for herself again, but caught that thought and repented, remembering all the times the Lord had supernaturally provided for her and her parents in Africa. *My God shall supply all my need according to HIS riches in glory in Christ Jesus.* Hallelujah! That familiar peace engulfed her again as she watched David walk down the hall. She punched out the numbers to call her mom.

After they hung up she picked up a magazine and was looking at all the strange people with heavy makeup, tattoos, piercings, high, high heels, short, short dresses. How did satan gain so much control over people? How did satan convince an entire generation of women that it was okay to look like hookers and it was okay to kill their babies? But she knew that before Jesus returned, satan would try to pull out all the stops and many, many people would be deceived. Satan knew his time was short.

She wished she had brought in her book bag. At least she could be reading something of value. She just decided to use this time to talk to God and pray for Jason. Eventually she saw David come back. He had three huge shopping bags and his workout bag. He pulled out a pink toiletry kit with toothpaste, brush, soap, deodorant, etc. and handed it to Kristi. He also handed her the three bags.

"There's a bathroom around the corner if you want to clean up a little. I saw some clothes in the gift shop that I thought you might like too."

"Oh, David. I can't accept these; I have no way to pay." Remembering the food he had brought to them, she said, "You've done so much already."

He put his finger to her lips. "Shhh. Just accept my gifts. Now go! I'll be in the other bathroom down the hall."

She found the secluded bathroom and took off her clothes down to her slip. She washed her face and around her body, brushed her teeth and brushed her hair. She found baby powder that she sprinkled over her and hand lotion. He had provided everything she could possibly need.

She then pulled out one of the dresses. It was a powder blue dress that fell just at the knees on her. It had a tiny black belt that circled her waist. It fit perfectly! She looked at her shabby shoes and tried to clean them as much as possible. She looked further in the bag and found matching cotton sweaters, hair bows and bands. She used the black hair band to hold back her hair, and noticed more clothes in the second bag. The third bag had three pairs of shoes – ballet flats like she liked – black, white and pink. She couldn't believe it. These were the most gifts she had ever been given at one time. She put on the black pair and they fit perfectly. How did he know her shoe size? How did he know her dress size? She tried to see as much of her image as possible in the small mirror, but she knew she had to look better than when she arrived. She didn't mean to seem vain; she just wanted to look nice around David.

She still had not told him about her dream and she couldn't wait. Would he feel the same or was this wishful thinking on her part?

He was standing in the waiting room in the shirt he had changed into. He looked better also. When he saw her, he gasped. She was so beautiful.

He went to her and touched her hair – something he had wanted to do so often – and said "You're so beautiful," and leaned down to kiss her. She turned her head. She was so shy with him. And she wanted to kiss him more than anything.

David was a little disappointed that she wouldn't kiss him, but he was happy that she was here with him. He held her as long as he could before it began to feel strange to her.

He said, "You stay here; I'm going to go buy the Robinsons' some dinner and I'll bring us something back as well."

He finally came back with several bags (in case other people showed up) and told Kristi that the Robinsons still did not know about Jason's condition.

They ate hamburgers, fries and drinks and continued to wait. Kristi started yawning. (It was about 11PM by now.) David had seen pillows and folded blankets on a cart just outside the linen area. He said, "I'll be back."

He came back with two pillows and a cotton blanket. He cut out the overhead light, then sat on one end of the small sofa. He put one pillow on his lap, one behind his head and told Kristi to lay her head in his lap.

As she put her head in his lap, he covered her with the blanket. She was asleep in no time. He just watched her as the hours passed. He did text his mother that they were still at the hospital, and took a picture of Kristi sleeping which he sent to her as well.

Around 3:00AM, the Robinsons came in and said that Jason was to stay overnight for observation. He had a broken arm, but x-rays showed no other signs of damage, but they wanted to monitor his condition through the night. If he still seems better in the morning, then he should be released tomorrow. "Thank you both for helping us through this."

David and Kristi hugged them and David said, “Well, we’ll come by in a day or so to check on him.” They all hugged again, thanked him for the prayers, the food and the company and then left.

David and Kristi walked hand in hand to the truck. He couldn’t believe it. Everything seemed to be coming together. It may have come through tragedy, but it was there all the same.

At her house, David lifted Kristi from the seat and prayed this would become a regular ritual. Then he walked her to the door and put the clothes bags and the food bags around her.

She thanked him again and looked into his eyes. He leaned down to kiss her again, but she turned away so he kissed her cheek. He would take whatever he could get.

“I’ll see you tomorrow Kristi. Father, thank You for Kristi. Please bless her, protect her and show her Your Will.”

He turned to leave, but turned back to her. “I love you Kristi.”

Still looking at him, she nodded and went inside. She put the food in the bare-again fridge and took her clothes into her room. She pulled out two more dresses – more beautiful than the one she was wearing. She felt like a princess. Why didn’t she let him kiss her? She WANTED to kiss him!

She hung up her new dresses in her almost-empty closet. She took off her new dress and put it with the others. She would wear the pink dress tomorrow. She was so happy and decided to tell him about her dream tomorrow. She put on his shirt again to sleep in. Somehow it made her feel safe. She didn’t even want to wash it because it smelled like him and she wanted to hold onto that for as long as possible.

16 THE TRUTH

He got home around 4:00AM and saw his mom had waited for him. He told her everything that had transpired with Jason, his family and Kristi.

"Did you get any sleep at all at the hospital?"

"No, I just watched Kristi sleep. She makes me so happy, mom." He finally wanted to tell his mother everything, but that would have to wait. He was so tired.

"Well, cut off your alarm; you don't have to go to school tomorrow. You sleep in and I will send in your excuse."

"Well, make sure you wake me around noon, so I'll have time to get ready and pick up Kristi after school."

As she watched him leave, she said a prayer: *"Thank You, Lord, for answering my prayers for David and Kristi. Please guide them both to do Your Will. I love You, Father."*

As asked, she woke him up at noon and he jumped out of bed for the workout. He worked out for an hour and rehearsed what he would say to her when he picked her up. He was running a little late and didn't want her to get on the bus and miss him. If he did miss her, he would go to her house anyway – he now felt very comfortable around her parents. In fact, he already loved them.

He hugged his mom when she entered the kitchen. She laughed and started asking questions about Kristi.

"Mom, I know she likes me. She lets me hold her hand; she lets me put my arm around her, and I've seen other guys try to put their arms around her, but she pushes them away. She lets me do these things, but she won't let me kiss her. She turns her head. I don't know from one minute to the next if I really have her or not. It does seem like she's finally returning my affections somewhat. What should I do?"

"Remember the video you showed me of her in the Library?" He nodded. "Well, remember when she realized you were there, she gasped. She kept looking at you and she started breathing hard. Didn't you see that? David, women don't react like that unless they really LIKE someone or they FEAR someone – and I know she doesn't fear you."

"I hope not," remembering the look of fear from the encounter with Zach.

"If she really likes you, when you pick her up today, she will have been missing you all day, so that when she does see you, she'll be happy and ready, if you know what I mean. As soon as you see her, don't say a word. Just hold her and kiss her. Go straight in. You need an answer NOW. If she doesn't like you, she won't let you kiss her, and you'll have your answer – even if it is a painful one. But somehow I think you will find a very different Kristi than last night."

"Oh, Mom, I hope you're right. That is exactly what I will do. Then we could go somewhere and talk and I can tell her everything the Lord has told me."

Laughing she said, "So if I see you home for dinner, that will be a bad thing. Just give this to God, David. He knows what's best."

"I know Mom. You're absolutely right. I love you Mom." He kissed her and ran up the stairs to shower.

* * * * * * *

At school, Kristi was wearing the pink dress David had bought. People were complimenting her and she felt wonderful. Bryan made a point to compliment her. "Wow, Kristi. You're the prettiest girl in this School."

She blushed and kept looking for David. She couldn't find him and looked in all the usual places. Sasha was also out. At her locker, Felicia was reading one of Sasha's texts and made a production out of it so that all could hear.

"Sasha says that David came over early this morning and they went swimming in her pool. Her parents were out of town, so she and David were swimming in the nude and making love all morning. She just texted me a picture of the tattoo David had gotten of Sasha's name. She says it's on his back shoulder."

Then she laughed again. "Sasha says his next tattoo will be her initials over his heart." Laughing, Felicia showed the picture to the others standing around her.

Kristi's heart sank as she stood frozen at her locker. "Oh God, this can't be true. Has he been lying to me all along? How could I have been so taken in? How could I have fallen for his charms? He has played me like a piano. How could he deceive me so? I feel so used." She was just not used to this kind of twisted behavior. Now she was glad she wouldn't let him kiss her. She wanted to cry, but she fought the tears. Her heart was broken. How could he seem so sweet and sincere, but be such a reprobate and a . . . liar? He just used girls as a game.

She stood frozen at her locker until the last bell rang. She had tests scheduled in the testing lab, but didn't want to see anyone and didn't want anyone to see her. She made up her mind. She would NOT finish this school year; in fact, she was never coming back to this school. She would go directly to Africa as soon as possible. Then she remembered how poor her parents were. Who was she kidding? She couldn't afford a ticket to the next town, let alone Africa! She would probably just quit school and get a job to help them. She knew Africa would have to be put on hold for now. But whatever awaited her, she could never face him again and she would never come to this school again. She would ask her mother to return all the clothes and things he had given her.

Then she remembered she had almost told him about that dream she had and was now so thankful she had not. If she had, he would have used that dream to take further advantage of her. She felt like such a fool. Her heart was breaking, and she was having trouble breathing. She went to the Library, pulled a chair around "their table" and sat until school was out. She just wanted to go home and cry. If the librarian came around to question her being there, she would just walk home. Fortunately, she was left alone until the bell rang for the end of school. She rushed down the Library stairwell before anyone could see her tears.

* * * * * * *

What a beautiful day to get some video. Bryan had already set up his tripod to get some shots of departing students. He had been taking pictures and videos all year for an end-of-year video and pictures for the web site and Year Book. He panned around and videoed David standing next to his Hummer, looking like he had just stepped out of GQ Meets Marine Muscle Magazine. What was he doing here? He wasn't even at school today, so he must be here for Kristi. *God, please help these two get together.*

He zoomed in and said, "Ladies and gentlemen, this is one of the most popular guys in this school and he's a dedicated Christian. There are so many in this school that he has helped and led to Christ – including me!" Trying to sound like an announcer, he said, "And ladies and gentlemen, you are looking at the next Prom King of Hillcrest High."

Voting for Prom King and Queen would be next week and he intended to send out this video clip to help David get elected, but he also knew David didn't have any real competition, so his election was pretty much a given.

About that time he saw Kristi walking to her bus wearing a new pink dress. Wow. She looked great! He turned the video onto her and said, "And Ladies and gentlemen, this is 'Pretty in Pink' Kristi Day – the sweetest and most beautiful girl in this school – who SHOULD be voted Prom Queen. She has also helped so many people this year – even though she's been the target of intense bullying, people never knew because Kristi has never said an unkind word about anyone. Beautiful inside and out!"

He knew most people would probably vote for Sasha – the biggest fake in the school, but people were sheeple and didn't use logic a lot of times. An idea was forming. Still trying to sound like a professional commentator, he said, "Our vote should not be wasted on the undeserving. Use common sense, people!"

His camera followed Kristi as she headed to the bus. "Yes, our next Prom Queen – and pretty in pink!"

She was completely lost in thought – just wanting to get home. She would fall into her mother's arms and cry and cry and tell her everything.

She thought she heard someone call her name, but she didn't want to talk to anyone and just kept walking. She kept trying not to cry – not until she got home to her mother.

She heard it again louder. She looked to her left and gasped. There he was standing next to his Hummer, calling to her. Slowing down, her feet turned, seemingly on their own volition, and headed towards him. Her mind was fighting this, "No, I can't see him. I don't have the strength to fight him. *God, please help me. I can't do this."*

She was getting closer, "It's not too late. Run to the bus. You do NOT have to talk to him." But part of her wanted to be with him like they were last night. She wanted his arms around her again. Her feet defied her and kept walking towards him.

As she got closer, he stepped towards her and wrapped his arms around her as she dropped her bag and lifted her arms to him. He leaned down and kissed her so gently. This time she did not turn her head. Then his arms tightened around her and he kissed her with increasing passion. She returned his kisses with a hunger and passion she had never felt. All thoughts that had plagued her earlier were pushed into dark corners of her mind. He finally looked into her eyes and, smiling, said, "I missed you today."

Any strength she had was completely gone. She could only nod to him.

Silently he was thanking his mother. She was right about her missing him. He said, "Let's get out of here."

Completely drained, Kristi said, "My legs don't work; you're holding me up."

David said, "Well that's no problem." He picked her up and put her in the Hummer. As he buckled her in, he leaned down and kissed her again.

He threw her bag in the floor, jumped in and drove off. *"Thank You Lord! Wow, just wow and THANK YOU!"* he prayed.

* * * * * * *

Bryan had the entire episode on video with many parts zoomed in for the most fantastic close-ups. He had been positioned perfectly at an angle best for capturing their meeting. He KNEW he had something incredible and couldn't wait to get home to see in full screen what he had captured. Finally, those two have gotten together and he knew he had been instrumental in the union. He felt proud. *"God, please bless them and protect them. You're so good, Holy Father."*

17 TOGETHER?

As David was driving, Kristi was awash in the same happiness she had felt last night. How could she doubt him? She put her hand behind his head and felt it was wet along with his shirt collar. Suddenly, all of Sasha's texted words came back to her. They had been swimming all day and probably had not been out of the pool long, so his hair and collar would be wet. But she remembered what Reecy had said about David and Sasha. She had to know the truth.

Knowing in her heart she could not be with him if he was a liar and defiled she said, "David, please go to the park. I need to ask you something."

Awash in the incredible happiness of having her with him, he complied. He pulled into their favorite area with the concrete picnic table. He lifted her out and sat her on the table top. He leaned down to kiss her again, but she held out her arms as a barrier.

"David, I've learned some things. I . . . I just need to know . . ." She needed to ask smart questions with direct answers, not questions that could be ambiguous.

"Ca . . .Can you tell me where you've been all day?"

Confused with the question he said, "Well, I was sleeping until about noon, then got ready to come get you."

Seeing the concerned look on her face, he said "Honey, what is it?"

"Your hair was wet. Have you been swimming?"

He thought, how did she know I have a pool? "No, I just got out of the shower and ran here to pick you up."

"But David, I was able to get enough sleep and make school today."

"Yes, but you slept in my lap last night and I just sat and watched you. I didn't sleep at all – just watched you. I didn't get home until around 4 AM."

"Oh."

She remembered the tattoo and with complete embarrassment, she said. "David, c- . . . could you please remove your shirt?" If the tattoo was there, then everything Sasha had been saying was true. If it wasn't . . .

Looking even more confused, he started unbuttoning his crisp oxford shirt. He was so glad he had worked out before he came; he knew his muscles would be pumped and he wanted to impress her. He had not put on a t-shirt. He didn't mean to be vain about his physique, but he worked out too hard for it not to matter. With the oversized shirts, he did try to cover it up as much as possible. When he opened his shirt, she gasped. She had not expected him to be so built. He was happy that she seemed impressed, but he knew he also had to keep his vanity in check.

Remembering that Felicia said the tattoo was on his shoulder, she said, "C . . . Can you turn around?" She was so embarrassed to ask him, but she had to know. She was holding her breath. This was the moment of truth.

Still confused, but totally enjoying every minute of this, he turned completely around (making sure that every muscle was flexed) and said, "Do I pass your inspection Ms. Day?" He resisted the urge to muscle-man pose and laughed as he reached for her again.

Still, she brushed him away. She was so relieved that there was no tattoo, but she was still confused. Sasha had obviously lied about the tattoo, but was she also lying about dating David?

"Kristi, what is it?"

Finally, she had to know. "Are you dating Sasha or have you dated Sasha?"

"Sasha? What brought that on? I do not like that girl. She's a bully and a big flirt. I wouldn't date her if she were the last person on Earth. Where is this coming from?"

"Well . . ." she stammered, "Sasha was also not in school today, but she sent pictures to Felicia of you and her in her pool, swimming in the nude. She also sent pictures of her name tattooed on your shoulder." She was too shy to mention the sex part.

David threw back his head and laughed out loud. "Did you see these 'pictures?'"

"No, but Felicia was showing them to Roxanne."

"Honey, she's telling lies, plus she's a PhotoShop expert. That's how she creates these pictures. She's been lying about me all year and the year before that and producing her "pictures" as proof. My mom even had a talk with her mom about the rumors she was spreading. She hasn't stopped, though, and we're powerless to do anything about it. Kristi, she knows how much I like you. She watches every time we're together and she knows if we start dating, then her lies will be revealed. Ever since you started school, Sasha keeps looking at me, but every time she does, I'm looking at you. She's not stupid. That day you saw me whisper to her, I was telling her in no uncertain terms to stay away from me. My exact words were: 'Get out of my face and stay the hell away from me.' Remember, she left very quickly after that and you haven't seen her around me since then, have you?"

"I just don't know what to believe. I have no experience with this type of thing. Sasha is so beautiful and I understand that things are very different and looser in America and I'm just a novice. But I'm not stupid either. I've never kissed anyone, but when you kissed me . . . I do know that that was the kiss of a very experienced person."

She was looking directly into his eyes to detect any sort of discomfort. She *had* to know the truth. He lovingly took her hands and said, "Kristi, I've never dated anyone in my life, let alone kiss them. I made a vow to God that I would wait for whomever he wanted me to have and I have kept that promise. You're the first girl I've ever kissed and hopefully the last."

Could this be true? Her heart flooded with love for him again but was still confused. "But that kiss was so, so perfect. You had to have experience."

"Kristi," he said moving in closer, "I've kissed you a thousand times in my mind."

Her heart melted and she fell into his arms. He held her tightly for several minutes. He felt this was what she needed from the harrowing events of the day. He couldn't believe he was finally holding her. She finally looked up at him and he kissed her again.

To further reassure her, holding her at arms' length, he looked straight at her and said:

"Number one: I have never dated anyone – especially Sasha.

Number two: Until about 15 minutes ago, I have never kissed anyone.

Number three: I would never in a million years get a tattoo.

Number four: I promised God that I would wait until I was married to have sex, and I'm sticking to that promise, and

Number five: I will never lie to you and I will never hurt you.

Kristi, you mean the world to me. I felt that about you from our very first encounter. I've never felt like this about anyone and I don't want to do anything to hurt you. Don't you feel like God put us together?"

She was still listening to him.

"Kristi, do you believe me? Because we can't have any kind of worthwhile relationship if one person doesn't trust the other."

In her spirit, she *knew* he was telling her the truth – and not just because she *wanted* to believe it. "Yes, David. I do believe you."

Her heart was filled with love for him. He was undefiled and God had given her the man of her dreams. He had kept His promise to her. She had never known such happiness. Then she thought about how close she had come to rejecting it all because of Sasha's lies. God had led her to His Truth. Hallelujah!

They held each other and said silent prayers thanking God. He was so good to them both. A warmth enveloped them as they held each other and could feel His Presence. *"Thank You JESUS!"*

Finally, he said, "Are you hungry?"

Not having eaten all day, she said "famished."

They had burgers at JJ's Diner, then drove around. She told him about her dream and he showed her his journal with the details of his dream – the *exact* dream she had had. She was still in awe of how God had led them together. *"Thank You LORD!"*

Tomorrow being Saturday, they talked, held hands and kissed until almost midnight. He kept kissing her. He knew he should stop, but he was so excited about being with her and FINALLY being able to hold her. He finally knew he should get her home and was still in awe that God had answered so many of his prayers. *"God, thank You for Kristi!"*

* * * * * *

When Kristi got home, she was putting the JJ's leftovers into the fridge and noticed it was almost bare again. What was she going to do? *"Lord, please help my parents. You know what they're going through and You said in Your Word You've never seen the righteous forsaken nor His seed begging bread. Thank You Father for providing all our needs."*

She went to bed with excitement because David was picking her up for lunch and a later date, and her parents (and Molly) had food for tomorrow. They also had plans to take Jason's homework by his house and to check on his progress.

18 JASON'S HOUSE

David took great care in looking his best today. It was almost May and school would be out soon and when they went to school on Monday, everyone would know that he and Kristi were together. He wouldn't hold anything back. He would hold her hand, he would put his arm around her; they would eat lunch together and be together between classes. He was so proud and the happiest he'd ever been in his life. *"Thank You, Holy Father."*

* * * * * * *

Bryan could not believe his luck. That video looked like a professional job – like something out of a movie. No edits necessary. He had zoomed in at just the right moments with the camera adjusting perfectly for one of the most romantic kisses in history! He took care to create the e-mail he was sending to all but a select few. It read:

Dear Fellow Students: As you know we will all vote for Prom King and Queen next week – and everyone thinks they already know who will be voted Prom Queen. Well, I offer you a different choice. Take a look at this video and you tell me who should be our Prom Queen (with whom our coming Prom King is apparently in love) – the most beautiful and sweetest girl in our school – Kristi Day! She may not dress like a queen, but her heart is like a queen and you all know it. Do we really want some snob representing our school? I know you will vote in the right way.

He said a prayer and hit SEND – which went to everyone in the school – except David, Sasha, Felicia and Roxanne. Kristi didn't even have an e-mail.

* * * * * * *

He drove up and saw Kristi and her mom sitting in the porch swing waiting for him. He jumped out, gave Kristi's mother some cookies his mother had made and she hugged him. He wrapped his arms around Mrs. Day and kissed her cheek. He then gave Kristi 24 pink roses. He couldn't wait to get her alone so he could wrap his arms around her, but he wouldn't be kissing Kristi on the cheek. Hallelujah! He wanted to shower her with so much. There were so many questions he wanted to ask her. *"Thank You JESUS!"*

David's mom had packed them a lunch which they took to their favorite picnic table in the park. She had thought of everything. Sandwiches, veggies with dip, cookies and water with lemon. A beautiful floral tablecloth and matching napkins and even a small glass and flowers for ambiance. They took it all and put it on "their" table. He sat next to her instead of across from her; he just wanted to be as close as possible. She seemed to want that too. Hallelujah!

They instinctively reached for each other's hands to join in prayer in blessing the food. They both felt just so right when they prayed together. After the picnic, they sat around and talked and kissed, but realized it was getting late. They re-lived scenes they had shared. What were you thinking when the storm hit and you turned to me? Why did you leave so suddenly in the Library? They talked for hours. (And kissed and kissed.)

They still needed to drop by Jason's house to deliver his homework. When they pulled up to his house (which was not located in the best neighborhood), he was waiting on the porch. His arm was in a sling and he seemed to be in a great mood. David said it was the painkillers. They went inside and talked to him, his mother and his little sister. Then Kristi remembered his homework in the back seat of the Hummer. David was telling Jason that he could have his old bike plus a bunch of gear he still had.

Jason said, "Your Cannondale?"

David said, "Yes, and I've got a lot of bike gear to go with it. Plus, I've outgrown my riding gear, so you can have that too."

Kristi said, "David, I left his homework in the Hummer; I'll go get it." He watched her as she left. He was so happy. Never in his wildest dreams had he ever thought . . . "Thank You LORD!"

Kristi bounded down the steps and almost had to climb into the back seat, but at least the back seat had a rubberized step she could use. The homework had fallen on the floor and she was about to lean down to pick them up when she heard tires squealing around the corner. She looked up just in time to see a white truck within 30 feet of where she sat. Her heart stopped. It was Zach with a cast on his left arm and he was looking straight at her! (She didn't realize that David's Hummer windows were tinted and he couldn't see inside.) She then saw him point a gun at the house, shoot several times and peel off. She heard screams inside, but sat frozen in the seat. All the fear from the stairwell episode came flooding back. She couldn't breathe. Suddenly David flung open the door and jumped in next to her.

"Kristi, are you okay?"

She grabbed David and clung to him. She was trembling uncontrollably. He held her so tightly.

"It was Zach. David, it was Zach. He looked at me. I thought he was going to shoot me. It was Zach."

David sat in shock as a flood of information bombarded his mind. Then he remembered the truck that hit Jason. That truck was headed for Kristi before Jason got in the way. The driver was Zach. Now it all made sense. *"God, thank You for protecting Kristi. Please help us Lord."*

He pulled out his phone. "Dad. Zach just drove by Jason's house and fired some shots. Call the police. Can you come by? Also, the truck that hit Jason was Zach too. Dad, he was trying to kill Kristi that day, not Jason."

"Where are you?"

"I'm sitting in Samson with Kristi."

"Is she okay?"

"Yes, a little shaken."

"Can you go back in and calm the Robinsons?"

There was no way he was leaving her. "Dad, I don't want to leave her and she's safe in this Hummer."

"Okay, just stay there until the cops arrive. Just call them from Samson. Tell them to get to the back of their house."

Then Kristi screamed. "David, my parents. If he knows where I live, he will try to hurt my parents."

"Dad, did you hear that?"

"Yes, call them NOW and tell them to get to the back of the house until the police arrive. I'll be there in 10 minutes. Just stay in the Hummer."

Kristi looked at David, "Aren't we sitting ducks in this Hummer? This Hummer won't stop those bullets."

"Samson will. It's bullet proof."

Kristi was stunned. What else would she learn about David? Did he really have all this power? Who was his father, really? It was all so strange.

David called Kristi's parents and told them what had happened. "The police will be there in a few minutes. Just get in the back of your house, preferably in front of a dresser, and wait."

He then called the Robinsons, still in the house, and told them the same thing. He told them to call Mr. Robinson at work for him to come home.

David's dad was there in no time. He jumped in the front seat of David's Hummer and closed the door. He looked at Kristi. "Kristi, everything will be okay. We handle these situations all the time. David, I've got the police at Kristi's house getting her parents. I want you to take Kristi to our house, then go help her parents pack some things because they won't be able to go back there until we get this guy. They can stay in our guest suite. They may be scared, so try to calm them as much as possible. Call Helga and tell her the situation to get the guest suite ready. I'll call your mom."

He looked at Kristi again. "It will be okay Kristi. Don't worry. Your parents will be safe."

He then went in to see the Robinsons and wait for Mr. Robinson.

David's heart was bursting with joy. His father wouldn't let just anyone stay at our house – not even their distant relatives. A day ago, he hadn't known whether he would ever be with Kristi and now they had had their first date and she would be living in his house. Abundantly, exceedingly above all that we ask. *Thank You JESUS!* He wanted to shout from the housetops.

Pulling into the driveway of Helga's house (really our house, but Helga and Norbert lived there full time), he punched in the code for the gate to open.

Kristi said, "Oh David. Your house is beautiful."

"That's not our house. Well, it is, but we don't live there. We just use it occasionally."

He then drove around back and kept driving through a cypress-lined drive before they came to another gate with a guard house. When Jack saw David's Hummer, he activated the gate to open. David stopped at the gate. "Jack, this is Kristi."

"Well, hello Kristi. I was wondering when I would get to meet you. Welcome to chez Everett."

This man acted like he knew all about her. "Thank you. It's nice meeting you also."

David drove through and came to a house, well a mansion really, that was one of the most beautiful homes Kristi had ever seen. She couldn't even see the entire house from her standpoint. They drove into a covered portico and David parked in an area that could only accommodate his massive Hummer. Kristi was taking in the breathtaking estate. "Oh my. You live here?"

"Yes, my grandfather built this. We're just caretakers and we only occupy one wing. And, just for the record, we NEVER let anyone come visit here; we always meet them in town or at the white house in the front."

“I’m honored. But why did you make an exception for us?”

He looked at her. She really didn’t know. He just said enigmatically, “It just seemed the right thing to do.” He loved her so much.

Helga was still in the kitchen getting bags and baskets ready for the Robinsons. His mom was already planning to set them up in a hotel safe house with goodies to help them cope with the situation. Anna came running in and hugged Kristi. Kristi couldn’t believe the love in this house. Anna was pulling Kristi in to show her her toys and Muffin, their little dog. Then Kristi remembered Molly. What would they do with her? They couldn’t bring her here.

David said, “Well, I’m going over to pick up Kristi’s parents. Is the guest suite ready?”

Helga said, “Yes, and we even have a little doggie bed for Molly in their suite.”

Kristi couldn’t believe this. How did they know about their little dog? And why would they have such compassion for these things? She felt the tears. She was so happy. *“God, thank you for these Godly people.”*

David pulled her into the foyer. He saw her tears – thinking she was worried about her parents. “I’ll be back as soon as possible. Don’t worry. Your parents will be safe and I will take great care of them.”

She reached out her arms and kissed him hard. “Thank you. I will be praying.”

* * * * * * *

David met the officers at the Days and ushered the Days into the back of his Hummer, informing them of the bulletproof nature. While Mrs. Day was holding Molly, he loaded all the items they had packed. Nothing had been packed in Kristi's room because it was located at the front of the small house. He shuddered to think about the night he had put her to bed. What if Zach had come back then? She would have been unprotected. But he knew that guardian angels were encamped about her. *Thank You, Jesus, for protecting my Kristi!*

The first thing he saw were the pink roses on her desk. He packed the card, but knew he would be buying her fresh roses every day. He opened her closet to find the familiar white blouse and denim skirt along with the other two dresses he had bought. He loaded all of those and turned back to her desk. There were several pictures of Kristi in Africa with her arms around different people. He picked up one with her arm around one of the biggest, blackest men David had ever seen. He could tell, though, that he was very good looking. She had the biggest smile in this picture and he suspected this was the famous warrior Samuel. He was at least a foot taller than Kristi, and he hoped this man would stay in Africa. He wasn't accustomed to feeling jealousy, but it was there all the same. There was also a very worn picture of Jesus holding a child. He knew this picture had a special place in her heart. He wrapped that picture in note paper and placed it in the side of the box. He then packed all the pictures and all the sparse desk items. She definitely fit the description of a Spartan – lean and basic. Remembering the Spartan phrase, he said "Molon Labe, Zach!"

He returned within the hour with Mr. and Mrs. Day in tow. They had already gone in to meet Helga (David's mom was at the hotel getting the Robinsons settled in) and David's little sister, Anna. Kristi hugged and kissed her mom and dad while Helga waited to show them the suite at the far end of the house. David brought in two cases. Apparently, the adjective Spartan fit the entire family. The suite had a huge bedroom with windows taking up an entire wall, a spa bath, a sitting area with a kitchenette and an outside patio. It even had a doggie door for Molly – perfect!

Kristi then went to find David. He was taking off some kind of pocketed vest (bulletproof?) and putting a firearm in a safe in the hidden room in the foyer. He closed the safe and closed a bookcase that served as the door to the safe room. He saw Kristi standing quietly waiting for him. He ran to her and kissed her. "I love you Kristi."

"I love you David."

He couldn't believe it. She LOVED him! He picked her up and swung her around the foyer. He pointed to the nautical starburst in the floor of the foyer. "I will remember this spot for the rest of my life. This is where my life begins." They kissed again.

"Thank you for taking such good care of my parents."

19 CHEZ EVERETT

When they entered the living area, Anna was sitting on Mrs. Day's lap. She already loved Mrs. Day. Anna was an affectionate child, but she didn't go to just anyone. She had a special knack for being able to discern good people.

Everyone seemed to be talking at once when David's parents came in. They both went to Kristi's parents and hugged them. Kristi was so glad they were making her parents feel so special. They told the Days about their early dating years, not knowing what to do with their lives. At church one Sunday night, the Days were preaching about their mission in Africa and the Everetts knew what they wanted to do.

"We have followed your mission for many years, but then we realized that our contributions to your ministry were being stolen by the ruling party in Mozambique. It was so corrupt, so all we could do was pray for you, which we do to this day."

Mrs. Day said, "That's more important than any money you could send."

Mrs. Everett said, "Sometimes the Lord would wake me in the middle of the night to pray for your ministry, so I knew He was looking after you. I also knew that I would one day meet you again. I'm just so thankful that I can return, at least in part, the favors your ministry has given me and my family."

Kristi's parents were clearly humbled by this display. They had no idea that their efforts had been recognized by anyone but the tribes in Africa they ministered to.

Mr. Everett said, "We didn't even know you were back. There should have been a homecoming celebration in your honor after all you've done for the Kingdom. You should have had a proper welcoming."

Mr. Day responded, "Well, we're not home yet."

Mr. Everett smiled because he knew he was referring to heaven. He really LIKED these people and knew he had made the right decision in inviting them into their home.

Everyone stayed up and talked until after midnight, and would have stayed longer, but Mr. Everett said he wanted to have a meeting around 11AM the next morning and then meet the Robinsons around 3PM. Kristi was asleep in David's arms and he told everyone that he would put her to bed. By this time the Days trusted him explicitly with Kristi. They all went to bed and his mom cut out the light – she instinctively knew that he would want the darkness.

He just held her until he fell asleep with his head next to hers. She eventually woke and asked David where she should sleep. He took her to his sister Beth's old room and turned down the bed. He pulled out one of Beth's nightgowns and gave it to Kristi. He kissed her goodnight and went to bed. He thought his life had been perfect before Kristi entered it. He never dreamed that happiness could multiply to this degree.

The next morning, everyone helped themselves to a buffet breakfast Helga had fixed and sat around and talked. Mrs. Everett noticed that Kristi was wearing the same dress as the day before. "Kristi, you don't have to wear that same dress. There are many dresses for you to choose." Kristi looked at her confused. Mrs. Everett grabbed Kristi's hand and took her back upstairs. She opened Beth's old closet where row after row of every kind of dress, blouse and outfit were displayed.

"Kristi, I was going to donate these to the clothing dispensary at the Sanctuary, but you can have anything you want in here."

"Oh, I couldn't take your daughter's clothes. She probably wouldn't like that."

She handed Kristi a picture of a pretty girl somewhere in a jungle, dressed in fatigues.

"THIS is what my daughter wears now. She is a missionary in South America. She fights like a guerilla and she wouldn't wear any of these clothes. She didn't want to wear them when I bought them. She's always been so different, so I would LOVE it if you would accept these. If there's something you don't like, just put it in these baskets and I will take those to the store at the Sanctuary."

Again, tears welled up in her eyes, "I don't know what to say. I can't believe how good you've been to us. How good you've been to Reecy. I don't know how to thank you."

"Kristi, just know that my son loves you and he is one of the finest Christians I've ever met. And I'm not saying that because he's my son. He truly is an incredible person. You'll see. He will never lie to you or hurt you or be unfaithful in any way. He's truly honorable. He has loved you since he met you and he's very blessed to have you as well. I am grateful that you and your family are a part of our lives now. One day you will know even more of how God put our families together, but this is not the time to reveal it."

With tears in her eyes, Kristi ran to Mrs. Everett and hugged her. "Thank you."

She helped Kristi pick out a feminine white eyelet dress with matching white ballet flats. She showed Kristi the hair clips and accessories. "Kristi, this is your room now and everything in it. We love you like you're our own daughter."

Mrs. Everett went back downstairs, but Kristi had to keep wiping her eyes before she could go back down and join everyone. *"God, thank You for looking after me and my parents. God, please bless these people."*

Around 11AM, Mr. Everett called everyone together and led them into a large conference room in the front of the house. Present were the Everetts, the Days, Jack (the guard), Norbert and Helga. Kristi sat next to David, who was holding her hand under the table. He still felt like he was dreaming, but at the same time concerned because he knew what his father was about to reveal. How would she react to that knowledge? *"God, please show us favor in this."*

When everyone was settled, Mr. Everett stood up and said a prayer. *"Holy Father, we thank You that we can come boldly to Your throne and give our thanks and honor to You. We ask You to anoint our words, to bless this meeting and to bless everyone here today, Lord. We know that all things work together for good to those who love the Lord and we do love You Lord. We thank You that you kept the Days safe, the Robinsons safe and You've kept us safe, Lord. We ask for Your holy guidance in everything we do. We give You the glory, honor and praise and we ask this in the name of Your precious son, Jesus Christ. Amen."*

My God. In Him will I trust.

Everyone said "Amen."

He continued speaking.

"What I'm about to tell you cannot leave this room. Do I have your solemn promise that anything you learn here today will be held in strict confidence?"

Everyone agreed.

"John, Ally, Kristi. This meeting is mainly for you. We have learned that Zach just recently bought that truck and paid cash for it. The previous owner had accepted the cash without bothering to get names and addresses of the buyer, so he didn't even know the name of the guy who bought it. Zach has not had the title changed into his name, nor has he applied for new plates. He's still in that window of time where he's driving around legally, but all of his activities are still traced to the original owner. He is not living at his last known address, so we are unable to track him. Consequently, you will have to live here until he is caught because he is very dangerous. He's already tried twice to kill you, Kristi, and has hurt an innocent person in the process. We need to catch this guy quickly before he hurts someone else.

Generally in dangerous situations such as these, we put people in some kind of protection program – we provide gated housing, different cars, different jobs, schools, etc. We provide everything they need until the perpetrator is caught. As such, John, we have paid your rent for the next three months, and alerted your landlord about this situation. However, you cannot go back there for any reason. If you need something out of the house, let us know and we will send in the guys who are surveilling your house. Your car will have to stay parked in the driveway and have the house lights on auto-timers to make it look as though you're still living there. So, if Zach tries anything, no one will be in danger. We have to do this so we can catch this guy. He is very dangerous.

But there is something else we want to discuss. Because of dreams my son has had and dreams my wife has had, I feel like the Lord is leading our families together. But, before you decide whether this union of our families is right for you, I must reveal some things to you for you to be able to make an informed decision about joining us. As you may have figured out by now, we engage in many covert operations that are sometimes quite dangerous. You know about our mission in helping families and individuals with various problems, but getting the people to the place for help can be fraught with danger. We work with the police, the military and special operations missions. In some cases, we have to refer these to the FBI to be transitioned into witness protection programs. I don't want to alarm you, but David is a paramedic, a police officer and an undercover agent in the School. He logs episodes of various abuses of power until we have enough for a case for trial or arbitration. That's how we were able to unmask the nurse who was doing so much damage in the community. My son has witnessed to several drug dealers in the schools and many have given their lives to Jesus. The ones who did not accept Jesus are now serving terms in prisons. He has also outed several teachers who were abusing the system in various ways."

Mr. Day spoke up. "Well, that does sound like it's filled with intrigue, but how can we possibly help you with that? We are getting up in years and I'm not much good with physically fighting someone, but we want to help your mission in any way we can."

"I'm glad you said that, John, and I'm convinced there are many ways you can help. As you know, I am over the mission board and we are looking for a new mission director. Actually we've been looking for almost a year, but I knew the Lord would send us the perfect person and I think that person is you. We need someone who understands missions and the challenges of being in the mission field. I would like to offer you that position. I would like for you to meet with the outgoing mission director tomorrow and as many days as you would like to spend with him. He will show you around and give you the rundown about our operational procedures. I want you to spend as much time with him as necessary, meet our staff and some of the in-state missionaries and let me know if you want to accept this offer. In the meantime, here is an employment package for you to read over before you accept."

"Richard, I'm almost 60 years old. Don't you think that's too old for your operation?"

"John, our current director is 86 and the only reason he's leaving is to move closer to his grandkids. So, no, age is not a criteria with us. In fact, we want someone with the experience and knowledge and wisdom that I know you possess. These missionaries will be continually looking to you for advice, prayer and guidance. We just want you to have a heart for missions, which I know you do, and to follow the teachings of Jesus, which I also know you do. So, the position is yours for as long as you want it. Just look over the package, both of you pray about it and let me know your decision."

He then turned to Mrs. Day. "Ally, my wife, with Helga's help, handles a lot of the behind-the-scenes tasks where she gets displaced families settled into new homes and/or safe houses. As you know, she loves to supply food for any occasion and helps victims with every need – food, clothing, jobs, etc. But sometimes families will need almost everything to begin their lives again – just like the Robinsons' situation. She counsels the parents or gets them to professional counselors, she helps the kids and gets them signed up for therapy – physical, emotional and spiritual – and is just there for them at every turn. She also runs the Sanctuary and all if its operational needs. I know she would love your help if you are willing."

He then turned to Kristi. "Kristi, David has told me many things about your compassion towards others – how you helped Reecy and her family – but it's only fair that you know how dangerous his job can be before you decide to join us. He's already told me of the harrowing adventures you've been through in Africa, along with all the problems you've had at the School. Are you ready for more drama? It can be very stressful if you're waiting for him to come home, but he's on some dangerous operation. What would you do in that situation?"

Without hesitating, Kristi said, "I would be in continuous prayer for his safety and protection, and I know God would take care of him."

Mr. Everett shared a knowing look with his wife. "David, I can see why you love her so much."

He then gave the Days some cell phones. "These phones have all of our numbers programmed in. They are not to be given to anyone and only a select few have our numbers. Please keep the call list separate from the phone. Jack, Norbert and Helga, you will have to update your phones with the Days' numbers. David, can you give them lessons on how to use them? Well, that's all I have for now. John, Ally, Kristi – do you have any questions?"

They all shook their heads "No."

"We will be meeting with the Robinsons at 3PM and I would like you to attend to give you some idea of what we do when we resettle a family. Their situation is typical of the type of family we help. But, in the meantime, let's just hang out until we go visit them."

"Thank you, Richard. This is incredible what you have accomplished. This is truly amazing."

"John, I don't know how to say this, but you and Ally are the reason any of this has been a success. Remember, you two are the ones who encouraged US so long ago. We thank YOU from the bottom of our hearts. God BLESS you!"

Mr. Day bowed his head and said a prayer, blessing everyone in the room and God's wisdom in all of their future missions. Then he motioned for his wife to follow him. "Honey, let's look over this package and pray about this. We need to know if this is what the Lord wants us to do."

She nodded and went to their room.

Mr. Day could not believe what he was reading. The employment package offered a starting salary of $160k per year, a $20k sign-on bonus, a company car, gas card and entertainment allowance. It provided fully paid health care for him and his family and even paid for college tuition for his children.

Mr. Day started crying. "Is this for real? A few days ago, I was worried out of my mind about how I was going to feed my family and keep a roof over our heads – and now we have this opportunity. What do you think, Ally?"

"I think this is a wonderful opportunity, John. And I would LOVE helping Rachel with the families in need. I would feel so useful. But let's pray about it and see what the Lord has to say."

They both knelt by the bed and prayed together. Really, it wasn't even about a decision. They both knew the Lord had led them to the Everetts and both thanked Him for this provision and continued miracles. *Thank You LORD JESUS!*

* * * * * * *

They all met with the Robinsons, explained the situation about Zach to them and how he had really tried to kill Kristi, but Jason, never expecting a truck to be driving down the sidewalk, had gotten in the way. Until Zach was apprehended, however, they still were in the line of fire. They were to be set up in a home in a gated community and Mr. Robinson was given a new car. Mr. Robinson explained how he had been fired from his job when he left to go home that Saturday, but Mr. Everett had already arranged for him to start a new job with one of his companies. They had to leave all of their furniture because their house was also being monitored in case Zach came back. The lights were put on timers. Their old car stayed in the driveway and it looked like people still lived there. They didn't know which house Zach would choose to hit, but both were being surveilled.

Mrs. Everett and Rachel were going to help Mrs. Robinson pick out new furniture for the house and get their daughter enrolled in a new school, new clothes – everything they would need to start over again. Before they left, the Robinsons, Everetts and Days gathered together and said a prayer of thanks and protection.

By Sunday night everyone was pretty tired. David and Kristi were in his room watching the Hallmark Channel. It was pretty cheesy, but David didn't care. He was holding Kristi and that was all that mattered. They both fell asleep, but some time during the night, Kristi woke up, covered David with a blanket and left to sleep in "her" room.

20 THE VIRAL VIDEO

When she came down the stairs the next morning, she was wearing a royal blue dress with matching shoes. She was also carrying a new book bag. He couldn't stop looking at her. She was so beautiful and he couldn't wait to show her off at school.

He had his arm around her when they walked down the hall. Everyone was smiling at them. David thought, "People are really freaking out about me and Kristi." He loved it.

What he didn't realize was that by now everyone had seen the video Bryan had made and they were all rooting for David and Kristi – except Sasha – who had been shown the video. She was absolutely livid and lashed out at anyone who spoke to her. Even Felicia and Roxanne were keeping their distance. All of Sasha's lies were finally coming to light.

David noticed that people were giving him odd smiles, but he attributed it to Kristi being on his arm. *"Thank You GOD!"*

Having taken all but three tests, Kristi spent most of her time in the Library, but all their free time was spent together so no one could really approach them. Bryan intentionally kept his distance because he was a little concerned about David's reaction when he DID find out about the video. Deep down he knew that David would probably thank him.

Everyone was also talking about the upcoming prom on Saturday night. The whole school knew by this time that David and Kristi were dating, so some girls asked Kristi what she would be wearing. Kristi was noncommittal because she knew her parents didn't have the money to buy her a dress. Even though her father had accepted the Mission Director position, he wouldn't be paid for a few weeks, and she would not ask Mrs. Everett. She had already given so much to her. She just hoped David wouldn't want to go.

On Wednesday everyone cast their votes for Prom King & Queen – except Kristi and David. They were oblivious to the voting activities and probably wouldn't have voted anyway.

Zach was still on the loose, but Mr. Everett knew it was only a matter of time before he was caught. They now had the license number and the truck description and a $10,000 reward for the officer(s) who apprehended him.

The Days were settling in with the Everetts without any hiccups. They had devotion in the mornings, prayed together at night and talked about Jesus a lot. Kristi was loving that her parents were eating well and being treated with respect. She knew this was from the Lord. And Molly and Muffin played together like puppies!

On Thursday night, the entire blended family was sitting in the family room all talking about different things. They all felt an incredible comfort being around each other. As Helga was leaving, the phone rang. She answered it and handed it to David.

"Oh, hi Coach Davis. Wow. I had forgotten all about that. Yes, I will help you. Oh, I'm bringing Kristi. See you then."

He turned to Kristi. "Honey, do you want to go to the prom with me?"

"Well . . . I, I really don't have anything to wear" she was careful not to embarrass her father about the lack of money . . . "plus it would be hard to find a dress at this late date."

Mrs. Everett said, "Kristi, have you not looked in Beth's other closet? Beth has many dresses that you could wear. Most never even tried on. My daughter was not really into girly things." She held out her hand to Kristi.

Laughing like a young girl, she said "Come on. Let's go try on some dresses."

Kristi grabbed her mother's hand and they all three bounded up the stairs, with David laughing at them as they went. He loved seeing her this happy. He could not believe his good fortune. *"Thank You Lord. You are so good to me."*

Mrs. Everett opened the closet, revealing a rainbow of long dresses and formal attire. Several were held up for Kristi's inspection. She couldn't believe it. She had never seen dresses so beautiful in her life. She pulled out several dresses that she liked and tried them on. Finally, she spotted a periwinkle blue satin dress with tiny sparkles and embroidery embedded throughout, Kristi knew that was the one. It had a sweetheart neckline, with cap sleeves (almost off the shoulder) and a flowing skirt. Both mothers hugged each other when Kristi was turning around for their inspection. It was perfect. There were also several yards of extra material. Mrs. Everett gave her the low heels that matched the dress. They were also a perfect fit. She felt like a princess and couldn't wait to show the dress to David. She said, "I'm going to show this to David" and turned to leave.

Mrs. Everett said, “Oh, no Kristi. Let’s surprise him on Saturday night.” She loved it that Kristi’s first thought was of David.” Here’s what we’ll do. We’ll all go get our hair, nails and makeup done on Saturday and we’ll make it a girls’ day out.”

They all agreed. It sounded like so much fun. Kristi could not believe how God was blessing her and her family. She then realized how God had not only answered her prayers about helping her parents, but He had also answered Kristi’s prayers about revealing David’s true character. *“Thank You Jesus.”*

* * * * * * *

After everyone had gone to bed, David gently knocked on his parents’ door. “Come in.” He tiptoed in and knelt by his mom. His dad said, “What is it son?”

“Mom, Dad. I want to ask Kristi to marry me. And I don’t want to wait. I know she’s the one. I want us to be married and then we can go to Africa together.”

“David,” his mom said, “Ordinarily, I would advise anyone your age to wait, but when your father and I were your age, our parents prevented us from getting married. We both KNEW God wanted us to be together, but we promised our parents to wait until after college to marry. In our opinion, we wasted four years of time that could have been spent serving God. So, yes, you have our blessing.”

They were sad to hear about them going to Africa, but from her own experience, Mrs. Day knew not to interfere with her grown son’s decisions.

“You know I have my own money from grandfather’s trust account, but I would like your permission to buy her a ring. I will also need you to help me find out a ring size.”

"Honey, we love Kristi. Buy her anything you want and I have known since you first told me about her that she would be my daughter in law."

"Thanks mom. I think I will ask her after the prom, but I will make sure I get permission from her parents before I do."

His dad said, "That's very wise son. Let me know what I can do to help."

While Kristi was upstairs getting ready for dinner, David asked to speak to her parents privately. He showed them the three-carat princess cut ring he had bought and asked their permission to marry Kristi. With tears in their eyes, they both said "yes" together and promised not to say anything to Kristi. He told them of his plans for after the prom. He hugged them both for a long time. He had never known happiness like this.

21 THE PROM

Early Saturday morning the three girls headed out for a day of beauty. All three had their hair, nails and makeup done and even had time for a relaxing lunch. When they got back home, Kristi went upstairs to take a bath and get ready. David came back in from a run and couldn't believe how great his mom looked. He twirled her around and threatened to throw her in the pool. They were all laughing and having a great time. Mr. Day couldn't believe how beautiful his wife looked. *"Thank you Lord, for my wonderful wife."*

David bounded up the stairs to get ready for the prom. He heard Kristi moving around in her room and couldn't wait to have her on his arm – knowing his plans for after the prom – and practicing what he would say. He was wearing a black tux, with a white tie and Helga had made a cummerbund and handkerchief from the same material as Kristi's dress. He felt fabulous and couldn't wait until the prom had ended. *"Father, please guide me.*

Show me the best time to ask Kristi to marry me. Thank You Lord."

Mrs. Everett and Kristi's mom went up to help her get ready. They put the dress over her head as it draped around her. They fastened the back and adjusted her hair which had been styled in long curls. A faux diamond clasp held her hair in the back. They both backed away and looked at her in awe. Her mother started to cry. Kristi wanted to cry because her mother was crying. "Baby, you are so beautiful." Kristi turned to the full-length mirror and gasped. How could this be? She already felt so loved and so beautiful. She never dreamed that within days, her life could be so complete. *"Thank You Father"* she prayed.

"Come on down when you're ready" said Mrs. Everett.

"I just want to pray a little. I'll be down in a minute."

The mothers had their arms around each other (knowing David's plans for tonight) and both women knew their families were about to be eternally linked and were very happy about their children getting married.

Everyone was gathered around waiting on Kristi when she appeared on the stairs. David looked up and could not believe his eyes. He had always known she was beautiful, but he was not expecting this vision. Mr. Everett was filming all of it. David took her hand and kept looking at her wondering how their wedding would compare to this. This clearly embarrassed Kristi but she was happy to be with him. He looked so good. Everyone was hugging each other because they all knew a secret except Kristi.

Mr. Everett and Mr. Day said prayers over them and blessed them before they left and David's father was letting him drive his SL500. Yes, life was very good.

As he was helping her into the car, he had the vision of her in his arms and now he knew what that meant.

They walked into the prom and almost immediately ran into Bryan who was attending with Reecy! Kristi hugged Reecy and asked her question after question. "Reecy, you look so beautiful. And your dress is incredible."

"Yes, David's mother gave me this dress. I've never had anything like it. I had forgotten about the prom, but Bryan called and asked me."

Kristi was so grateful to Bryan. He was always so thoughtful and Kristi knew he really liked Reecy.

Reecy kept looking at Kristi and said, "Kristi, you look like a movie star and I am so happy for you and David. I saw that video."

"What video?"

"The video Bryan took. You don't know about it?" Then she realized that she may have spilled the beans and quickly changed the subject.

Kristi and Reecy made their way to the Ladies' Room. They entered to find Sasha with her co-horts. Sasha gasped when she saw how beautiful Kristi looked.

As she left, she said, "Well, you can dress up a pig, but it's still a pig."

Kristi, not offended in the least, whispered, *"Lord, please help her. Open her eyes to Your Truth."* Reecy had heard it and was thankful that Kristi had not suffered hurt from her remarks.

"Kristi, she's just jealous because she will not be voted Prom Queen."

Kristi had forgotten about the vote. She knew David would win, but she secretly hoped whoever was voted Queen would be a good person. But inside she did feel a little anxious about it all. How would she feel seeing Sasha on David's arm? *"God, please give me the strength to endure this."*

They spotted David and Bryan talking. David rushed to meet Kristi. He grabbed her and pulled her to the dance floor. "David, I don't know how to dance except the dances we did in Africa."

"Honey, just follow me. I'll hold you," and they danced and danced. It all felt so natural.

At a certain point, Principal O'Reilly took the microphone and made a few announcements. He then stated that he would announce the votes for the Prom King.

"This vote was cast by you, the students, and represents the best of the best in this school. So, if you're ready, I proudly present the Prom King that will represent our school for this year – to a guy who excels in everything he tries. Not only that, he holds a 4.0 grade average and is an invaluable assistant to Coach Davis. I proudly present this year's Prom King of Hilcrest High to Mr. David Everett."

David gave an annoyed look to Kristi and didn't really want to leave her side. He decided that after they announced the Prom Queen as Sasha, he would step down and forfeit his crown to the next runner up. He made his way up to the stage where Principal O'Reilly put the crown on his head. The entire class erupted in applause. David felt ridiculous, but he patiently waited to make his announcement.

Returning to the podium, Principal O'Reilly said, "I just want to say before I make the announcement for Prom Queen that never in the history of the school has the voting been so decisive. The votes for both the Prom King & Queen were almost a unanimous vote – at an unheard-of percentage of 96% of the votes going to them. So, it is my honor to announce that this year's Prom Queen goes to one of the most beautiful girls in this school and was written on so many of your ballots . . .."

At this point Kristi saw Sasha making her way to the bottom of the stairs leading up to the stage. She tried to fight the disappointment, and yes, jealousy, of her standing next to David. Her anxious thoughts drowned out the speaker.

People started screaming. She didn't know what was going on. She looked up at David, who was smiling from ear to ear and he was holding out his hand to her. Reecy was pushing her toward the stairs and David was making his way to meet her. She looked at Reecy. Reecy said, "Kristi, YOU were voted Prom Queen." She must have misheard. "Go, go – they're waiting for you." Sasha was halfway up the stairs. David brushed past her, giving Sasha a strange look, but took Kristi's hand to join him on stage. She was truly shocked. He was holding her tightly.

Principal O'Reilly was about to place the crown on her head, but David said, "Principal – can I have that honor?"

"Sure."

David took the crown and placed it on Kristi's head. He heard in his spirit. *"Now's the time son"* and he knew what he had been directed to do.

Holding Kristi's hand, David went to the podium. "Thank you to my fellow students for truly selecting the best person for Prom Queen. She truly is the most beautiful person I've ever known. And Kristi, this school has voted you Prom Queen for the school, but I would like to vote for you as my queen." Taking the ring out of his vest pocket, he said, "Kristi, I've asked your parents' permission, and. . ." he knelt down in front of her as the entire congregation let out a collective gasp. The entire room was silent – every eye on Kristi and David.

"Kristi, will be marry me?"

Through her tears, she nodded yes, as he put the ring on her finger and rose up to kiss her with the same passion as the video playing on the screen behind them which Bryan had previously arranged to be shown.

They both looked at each other and whispered in unison, *"Thank You Jesus!"*

The entire school exploded in deafening cheers and applause. Their proposal was caught on video, and went viral. The music resumed and David and Kristi danced together on the stage, then went down to join their classmates. The rest of the night went by as a blur. Kristi couldn't believe any of this was happening. Was this a dream? If so, she didn't want it to end. *"God, you're so good to me. Thank You for helping me. Thank You for helping my parents, and thank You for helping me find the man You have given to me."*

* * * * * * *

As they walked through the doors of the house, they entered a darkened family room. As soon as they entered, the lights came on and cheers rang through the house. They were all looking at the ring David has bought and had already watched the Prom that had been live-streamed, so they knew everything that had transpired. Finally, David and Kristi watched Bryan's video and watched the proposal from the Prom. David then realized that God had planned that proposal. David couldn't have pulled off something so perfect in a thousand years. We serve a great big GOD! *"Thank You JESUS!"*

As the excitement died down, Mrs. Everett went to a large desk at one end of the room. She pulled out a bound sketch pad, turned to one of the drawings and handed it to Mrs. Day.

"What do you think of this, Ally?"

Mrs. Day looked at the drawing. It was the picture of her holding Anna the night they arrived.

"This is amazing. You captured our likenesses perfectly." She handed the picture to Kristi.

"You have amazing talent Mrs. Everett."

"Look on the back of the picture."

Mrs. Day turned over the picture. The date was almost exactly two years before. The two women looked at each other in astonishment. "B – But how did you know what I looked like?"

"I didn't," said Mrs. Everett. This was a vision I had before I was given instruction from the Lord.

"What kind of instruction?" asked Mrs. Day.

"A few years ago, I had a dream about building a house for a missionary couple. In the dream, I walked into the kitchen and saw Anna on your lap. The next morning, I drew the picture you're holding. I knew exactly how the Lord wanted the house built and furnished and I knew what the missionaries would look like. So we built the house and whenever I started to insert my own design and preferences, the Lord would redirect me and gave me deeper insight into the design. The house sat empty and I was concerned that I may have misheard my assignment. A few months ago, I asked the Lord if He still had someone in mind and I was told to be patient. When I entered the kitchen and saw Anna on your lap – just like in the picture – I knew the house was for you and John. It's just down the road, but still on this property. I would like to take you to see it tomorrow. If it meets with your approval, I would like to give you the deed to the house that includes 10 acres. It has a separate entrance from the main road, or you could use our more secure main entrance."

Mrs. Day started crying as Mr. Day and Kristi ran to her side. They were all crying and thanking God. Mr. Day said, "We didn't think anyone knew about us. And I didn't understand how we would make it with my working at Value Mart – and now look how the Lord has provided – exceedingly, abundantly, above all that we could ask for. Thank you so much."

Mrs. Everett started showing them pictures of the house and they planned to all go inspect it tomorrow. The pictures showed a pretty little cottage, perfect for two people, with a picket fence around a small yard and garden. The inside was painted a creamy yellow with white kitchen appliances. The master bedroom and bath were painted periwinkle blue – Mrs. Day's favorite color! Mrs. Day sat in silence, then looked at Rachel.

"Rachel, this is the home of my dreams. I know the Lord gave you this design for me, because He knew that this was exactly what I've always wanted. It looks perfect!"

Mrs. Everett said, "See how God has always planned for our families to be joined – even from when Richard and I first met you two. You both inspired us and we thank you for that. None of what we do would have been possible if not for you and your ministry." The Everetts and Days hugged and held each other for a long times. Tears flowed freely, but they were tears of happiness.

David went to bed feeling all the happiness and goodwill in his house. He never wanted this to end. God had supernaturally put the Days into his and his parents lives and ALL their lives were so much richer and blessed because of it. *"God, THANK YOU! Are You kidding me? I love You so much and I will serve you all my days. My KING! Hallelujah to the Lamb of GOD!"*

22 THE WEDDING

The last few weeks of school flew by quickly. Kristi was preparing for her wedding which she wanted to be very small. They were going to use the conservatory around the corner from Helga's house. It was a beautiful, open, white, wrought iron structure covered in glass, with flowers blooming inside and out. Her colors were pink and yellow. Her flowers were pink peonies, yellow daffodils and white daisies. Her dress was a modest, princess style all-over embroidered satin that was not as full as most wedding dresses. She wanted to be comfortable when dancing with David.

What a beautiful day it was for an outdoor wedding: warm, but not terribly so. A pleasant early June breeze blew in as the select friends and family members took their seats on either side of the walk leading to the gazebo. Sweet strains of classical music drifted through the crowd. I couldn't believe it; Kristi and I were finally getting married. I was so nervous. I wanted it to be over so I could be with her the rest of my life and at the same time, I didn't want this day to end. I felt something could still happen that would prevent me from being with her. Mom looked so pretty and I could tell she was so happy with this union. Kristi's mom was on the other isle and looked happy as well. I was dressed in a simple white tux with a white satin tie. Dad, as my best man, and dressed in a black tux stood next to me as we waited. Bryan stood next to dad.

Everything looked so beautiful in pinks and yellows and everyone seemed very happy. I silently asked the Lord to bless everyone who entered to make our day more special. Dad's SL500 convertible was parked in the front, decked out in ribbons with twisted coils of streamers and cans, waiting for our escape. 'Just Married' was painted across the small trunk area. As I stood there, I thought to myself how perfect and lovely everything was. The smell of fresh cut flowers filled the air. What was the holdup? *"God, please let this be easy. Please don't let satan pull any of his stunts. God, I know you put us together. Please help me get through this. You're an amazing God and I LOVE YOU!"*

Suddenly the music stopped, and all heads turned to face the far end of the walk. Anna and Bethany, dressed in matching pink satin dresses, walked down first dropping pink petals along the way, with Reecy following. They stood on the opposite side of me. The opening to the bridal chorus started to play. My heart was beating so hard. Then time stood still. She and her father were walking towards me and I could see the love in her eyes. I could not believe how beautiful she was. She wore a simple satin wedding gown with beaded embroidery throughout the entire dress. Rhinestones and pearl beads were sewn on her gown. She also wore a two-tier veil, with a matching crystal tiara. She held pink peonies, daisies and daffodils in her bouquet. Her dad held her arm and smiled at her as they reached where we stood. Her father, crying, kissed her on the check and walked her the final steps to me. This was beyond anything I could have ever imagined. She was so beautiful.

The pastor placed the Bible down before him. "Let us begin by offering thanks to the Lord on this wonderful day." We all bowed our heads and he prayed.

After the prayer was over, the preacher led us through our vows. It was now time for the exchange of rings. Dad handed me the ring and I slipped it on Kristi's finger. The pastor smiled and turned to Kristi. He repeated the question and received the same reply. I watched her take my ring from Anna, who looked so pretty in her pink satin dress. Looking into my eyes, she put the ring on my finger and gently squeezed my hand. Almost in a dream, I heard: "By the power vested unto me I now proclaim you husband and wife. You may now kiss your bride." I leaned down and kissed her because she was now mine. This really messed up my "perfect" five-year plan, but I was not complaining. This was more wonderful than anything I could have ever dreamed or PLANNED! *Thank You JESUS!* I was happier than I ever thought possible. I picked her up and twirled her around as everyone laughed.

We then all went to the conservatory where food, music and all good things awaited. We danced and danced. I didn't want to turn her loose, but Kristi danced with her father as I danced with my mother. I also danced with Kristi's mother as Kristi danced with Anna and Bethany. How could any man be so happy? We were to spend our honeymoon in my, no, OUR lake house. We danced again and then spontaneously, we both wanted to leave. As we reached the decorated Mercedes, Kristi threw her bouquet. Bryan was standing with his arm around Reecy, but she caught it like a boss. I opened the door for Kristi, put her dress around her and jumped in the driver's seat. The sound of the cans and streamers was like a clarion call: David and Kristi Everett are married. David and Kristi Everett are married. Hallelujah. *THANK YOU JESUS!*

Later that night with her lying in my arms, I remembered the vision I had received so many months earlier. Looking down at her sleeping, I knew this moment was that vision. Then I remembered one the first notes she had written me. “You are a very blessed man.” Yes, Kristi, with you by my side and Jesus at the helm, I AM a very blessed man.

23 ALANA

They spent their honeymoon in David's lake house. They just didn't want to go anywhere; they just wanted to be together. They spent all day in each other's arms and shared reading each other's journals. It was very strange how some passages were almost identical to the other's. There was so much to learn about each other. Every day, they prayed together, read the Word of God together and took communion. Day by day they realized that God had put them together and He had big plans for them. Consequently, they both started planning for the next adventure of their lives – Africa.

Kristi started noting flight times, prices, etc. Then charted out a to-do list and timeline. They would spend June and July with the families and try to get to the mission field for early August. They had to get shots to go, but Kristi would put that off until the last minute. Those shots made her very sick for about a day. Disgusting! But they were required in order to travel. Before when she was planning it brought a heavy sadness because she knew if she made it there, she would never have enough money to even come back to visit. So her leaving for Africa meant that it would probably be the last time she ever saw her parents. That thought always made her cry. But now, since being married into this wonderful family, she would have money to come back to visit. God had truly provided in a way that was above anything she could have asked for. David had tried to sit down and go over his financial status, but she just didn't care. Money was a necessary evil to her, but the world ran on it and she couldn't live without a little of it herself. David kept buying her clothes, but she told him she had enough. She had planned to only take three or four dresses to Africa. He bought her anything HE liked that he wanted to dress her in. She was afraid she was like a doll to him, but it seemed to bring him happiness, so she didn't protest too much. *"Thank You, God, for giving me such a loving, good and PURE husband. Your promises are yea and amen!"*

David walked in and threw the new Kristi Day Everett Passport on the table. It had come in the mail right on time. He opened it just to look at her picture and to wonder in amazement all that God had done to put them together as husband and wife. *"Thank You LORD!"*

They were to ship the supplies ahead of their arrival and hoped that the corrupt officials would not confiscate them. They were sending everything to Pastor Ison, who had the adjoining mission about 20 miles away from where they were to set up. It was a hole in the wall named Alana. They would fly into Mozambique where they planned to buy a Range Rover and many more items they would need for the setup and for the trip to Alana. She hoped the roads would be cleared enough for them to make the whole trip in the Range Rover, so she kept an eye on the Weather Channel for that area. They should be there just before the rainy season. Whatever happened, they knew God would provide.

They would wait to hear that all their supplies had been delivered to Pastor Ison before they would set out. They had already deposited money into his bank account because they knew he would have to pay off the officials in order to take possession of the supplies. Kristi knew Pastor Ison would try to win those officials to the Lord – then they wouldn't be asking for bribes from others. Yes, the world would be a much better place if people just followed the teachings of Jesus and lived for Him!

In the meantime, Kristi kept compiling items and checking off things from her list as they were boxed for shipment and put aside. Last on the list – shots and she immediately dreaded the thought of the resulting sickness from them.

* * * * * * *

One night, Dad-E (what Kristi called Mr. Everett) called David in the middle of the night for an emergency mission. Drug dealers had holed up in an abandoned warehouse, but had several young children as hostages. David grabbed his SWAT gear, kissed Kristi and headed out. Kristi got dressed to join her mom and Mom-E to see what was needed to help. Helga began baking. All the women were ready for action whenever Richard sounded the alarm. They prayed protection over the children, over the men and women in harm's way, and over the salvation of the perpetrators. They listened over the police scanner until it was moved to secure comms.

David jumped into his father's SUV and they drove to the site where they were joined by other SWAT members and what looked like the entire police force. A call was put into the Governor's office for backup if needed.

The SWAT team was already in place at the front of the warehouse. Richard drove around back to join the team he and

David were assigned to. There were several cars parked in the shadows that somehow looked out of place to David. Then he saw it. That white Ford they had been scouring the town for. He walked around to the back of the truck where his suspicions were confirmed. The plate matched the license number etched in his mind. David gave the signal for his father to join him. David said, "Dad, that's Zach's truck."

Now they knew the identity of the ring leader. Richard radioed to the SWAT team commander, explained the situation so he would have valuable insight into the words he spoke to negotiate with the leader who had taken the children.

The SWAT team commander took the bullhorn: "Zach, we know what you're facing and we can make a deal for something much less severe if you will release those children. Zach, if you do not want to end up in the morgue tonight, call this number to negotiate. Are you ready? 708-999. Call that number so we can talk."

He put down the bullhorn and waited. About two minutes later, the phone rang. "Okay Zach. Here's the way this needs to go down. You're going to let those kids walk out safely – with NO HARM coming to any of them – Do you understand?"

Zach: "How did you know it was me?"

"Zach, we've been following you for weeks. We have everything on video, so, really, there is nowhere for you to run. You're looking at a long, long time behind bars because the videos are irrefutable evidence of criminal activity. If we hear the first gunshot, we're storming the building and we will make sure you do not survive. But if you work with us, we will make sure that your inevitable jail time is significantly shortened. You haven't killed anyone, so this is not as bad as you may think. Just don't be stupid. Do the right thing."

They really had not been following him and did not have videos, but Zach was freaked because they knew his name, so he believed them.

We waited for several hours. The commander called Zach. "Zach, we can stay here as many days as you like. But with each passing day, the negotiation window diminishes. It's up to you, Zach. However you want to play this. The negotiation is still on the table, but it will be taken OFF the table in ten minutes. Govern yourself accordingly."

In a few minutes four children started running out of the warehouse. One of the officers grabbed one of the older children and the commander asked him if any other children were still in the warehouse. Jamal said, "No, everyone got out fine."

David and his dad's team went into action with the children. They held the kids and told them everything would be okay. The two smaller kids were given stuffed animals and cleaned up because they had wet themselves. David wrapped two of the girls in blankets and just held them in each arm. His dad looked at him and said, "Son, that look suits you."

David smiled and wondered about having kids with Kristi. They hadn't even talked about it, but he knew Kristi would be a great mom. He just didn't know how he would feel about sharing her right now. He loved having her all to himself, but he knew the Lord would keep blessing them both in whatever way He chose. Hallelujah!

David looked up to see Zach, Larry and Dean being led away in handcuffs. *"God, please reveal Yourself to them. Let each know that You are real and You are powerful and Jesus is the Way, The Truth and the LIFE – and no one come to You, Father, but through Him."* He knew if someone like Zach turned his life over to Jesus, he would be another Paul and probably become a mighty man of God.

The parents had been kept at a distance, but with the perpetrators in custody, they were given the okay to come around for their kids. The little girls ran to their mom who hugged them and cried. David was glad those little girls were loved.

Richard walked over to David, put his arm around him and said, *"Thank You, Lord for keeping us safe and thank You for my Godly son. Please bless him, his family and protect them. Thank You LORD!* I'm so proud of you David. I don't know how I will handle these situations when you and Kristi go to Africa. I might have to recruit Anna." They both laughed, but David felt a sadness because he wanted to spend as much time as he could with his father. What an incredible teacher and role model he had been his entire life.

They were all still waiting up when they came in. Kristi again met David in the foyer putting away his swat gear. She ran to him and kissed him as he twirled her around the nautical star. Life was so good. *"Thank You LORD!"*

* * * * * * *

Kristi kept packing and sending supplies to Pastor Ison. They would have to live in tents while the medical center was built. Theft was always a problem, but she planned to follow her father's example. Her father had hidden all medical supplies in a hidden underground storeroom beneath the floor. He always built hidden tunnels for easy escape and they had come in handy too many times to count. She had their tickets and everything packed and within a few weeks, they would leave for Alana by way of Mozambique.

The timeline had been pushed back because of fighting in the area. It was now early September and they needed to get to the mission before the rains came.

One morning David went to the main house for breakfast.

“Where’s Kristi?”

“She wasn’t feeling well, but she will be up here later.”

“What’s wrong with her?” his mom asked.

“I don’t know. She’s never been sick before. Gotta go, mom. I will call you later.” He kissed her on the cheek and headed out the door.

“Ally, are you thinking what I’m thinking?”

“No, she gets sick like that every time she has those shots. She’ll be sick all day, but like new tomorrow.”

Rachel was disappointed. She was really hoping Kristi was pregnant and maybe, just maybe they would decide to stay. She just couldn’t explain it, but she really didn’t want them to leave. She was already hearing reports of guerilla attacks around that area. She just didn’t have peace about it. When Kristi comes up here, I will talk to her about the attacks.

David was back up the next day.

“Hi mom. Could you please talk to Kristi. I want her to go to the doctor, but she won’t go.”

“Is she still sick?”

“Yes, she says she feels better throughout the day, but this is hanging on.”

About that time Ally walked in. Helga handed her some coffee just how she liked it.

“Ally said that Kristi always gets sick when she had those shots.”

David chugged down his coffee and started out the door. “Oh, she hasn’t had the shots yet; that will be next week.”

Rachel, Helga and Ally all looked at each and then broke into three YUGE grins. Rachel grabbed Ally's arm.

"Come on, Ally, let's go buy some tests, shall we?"

They were back within the hour. Ally called Kristi to ask about her "sickness." Kristi said she was feeling a little better.

Ally said, "Well, when you get a chance, we need you to come up here. We just want to talk about a few things."

Kristi walked to the house. She didn't like driving the golf cart because she really enjoyed walking in the woods and listening to the birds. She also got the benefit of the exercise. When she walked into the kitchen where all the women were gathered, they all hugged her and asked all at once how she was feeling. Kristi thought they were acting very strange.

Her mom said, "Kristi, did you get the shots for your trip yet?"

"No, momma. We won't get those until next week. I don't want to get them until the last minute. I do not like those things."

"Well, what do you suppose made you so sick the last few days?"

"I don't know, momma. Maybe something I ate."

They were looking at her very strange.

Finally Rachel said, "Kristi, we've put something in the hall bathroom we'd like you to see."

Bewildered, Kristi looked at them. "What is up with you guys?"

"Just humor us." They were all pushing her toward the bathroom. "GO!"

Kristi walked into the bathroom and looked around. A package had been opened and was displayed on the granite counter. "What is this?" She had never seen one of these things, but then suddenly realized what it was.

"No way!" She read the instructions, followed the instructions and waited.

They were all standing outside the bathroom when she emerged. Kristi was crying. The mothers and Helga were crying. About that time, Richard came home and saw them all crying in the hall outside the bathroom. He rushed over to Rachel, "Honey, what is it?"

Rachel handed him the strip, "Read this Grandpa!"

He looked at the strip; he looked Kristi. He grabbed her and twirled her around like David did.

"Does David know?"

Rachel responded, "He doesn't have a clue. He thinks Kristi has the flu."

Richard said a quick prayer, thanking God and blessing Kristi and David and this new life.

He said something all the women wanted to say, but didn't dare. "Kristi, you can't go to Africa now. This changes everything."

When he said those words, Kristi's heart jumped in agreement. Now she knew what had been bothering her. She had not been in God's will and now she knew what He wanted her to do – and it didn't include Africa.

She said, "You may be right, but David and I will have to pray about this."

He said he understood, but there were plenty of mission fields in Hillcrest.

* * * * * * *

She couldn't wait for David to get home. She had kept the test strip and put it in the hall bathroom at their house. She had made salmon croquettes with remoulade sauce (one of David's favorites) and a small salad for dinner. She wore the powder blue dress that he had bought her that night in the hospital. It was one of her favorites and every time she wore it, it brought back memories of their first real date. "God, thank you for my incredible life and my Godly husband. How could You bless me so much?" When he walked in the door, she ran to him and kissed him. She knew they would talk about his day but he would eventually make his way into the hall bathroom.

He kept talking about all the people he had talked to today and how many people needed help. He had gone by the Sanctuary to drop off some items at the store and had seen Reecy. Reecy had invited them over for Saturday night pizza and to watch the game. Bryan would be there to. Unbeknownst to David, Bryan had won many of his friends to Christ and had been having discipleship studies in his home. He had really become a serious man of God and had legitimately been called to preach. He had been awarded a scholarship to a local seminary and had gotten a part-time job as a security guard at that same college. He could even select his own hours to work around his class schedule. He was pleased that he could go to school and live at home to look after his mom and little brother. Unbeknownst to Bryan, Robert had arranged the scholarship and the part-time job at the seminary.

He and Reecy planned to marry after he graduated. She was planning on becoming a Christian child psychologist so she could help others with what she had experienced. Bethany was flourishing in the small school at the Sanctuary and her mother was improving by the day.

Kristi was cleaning up the dishes at the sink as she heard him walk down the hall. "God, thank You for giving me such a Godly husband." She waited and listened, but she couldn't hear a sound. She was drying her hands when she saw him standing just behind her. He was just staring at her. "Kristi, is this us?" She nodded her head yes.

He held her tightly. He didn't kiss her; just held her. She could feel him sobbing.

She thought, "Oh no, was he not happy about this. David, what's wrong?"

"Honey, nothing is wrong. Everything is so right. How can God bless us like this?"

"I don't know, but He's blessed a lot of people in just this same way."

He laughed, THEN kissed her again and kept holding her – Unspeakable JOY!

David ran around the house, "We've got to tell mom and dad and your mom and dad – and Helga and Norbert. Kristi, we've got to get a nursery ready; we've got to get nursery and baby things. Let's go shopping tomorrow. Oh, man, I've got to call mom."

He was already dialing. Kristi said, "David, they knew before we did."

"What? How did they know?"

Kristi told him the story of this afternoon. Then he looked at Kristi.

"Honey, we can't go to Africa now. I want to stay here to raise our baby – just like my parents decided to do with me and my sisters."

She nodded her head in agreement and felt an immense peace about cancelling the trip. She would inform Pastor Ison tomorrow and tell him he could keep all of the money and supplies she had sent. He could really use it too.

My God. In Him will I trust.

* * * * * * *

March came in mild, but windy. Kristi was due any day so they were on high alert. Both parents were beside themselves with excitement. Kristi was hoping their child would be born on March 5th because March was the third month and the number three is very important to God – Father, Son, Holy Spirit. And five is the number of grace. Around 4 AM on that date, Kristi woke up David to take her to the hospital. She just knew this was the day. They welcomed their first child into the world – Alana Katherine Everett at 7 AM – the number of perfection. Both parents and Anna were there for the birth. When the nurse brought in Alana, everyone laid hands on her and dedicated her to the Lord Jesus Christ and prayed the Aaronic blessing over her. *"The Lord bless you and keep you; the Lord make His face to shine upon you and be gracious unto you; the Lord lift up his countenance upon you and give you peace."* Yes, they were all very blessed. Thank You Jesus!

ABOUT THE AUTHOR

Any info about me is unimportant. We live this life with one goal in mind: Where will we spend eternity? Jesus made that extremely easy for us when He took OUR sins upon Himself and died for us. What greater love than when a man lays down his life for a friend. That's exactly what Jesus did for us.

Looking back now, I realize how empty my life had been before I found Jesus. I feel so sad for anyone who thinks a personal relationship with Jesus is not possible. I used to think that way too. When I truly started living for Jesus, I began to understand things that were beyond my comprehension before. I gained a peace and a JOY that were indescribable and I wouldn't trade it for anything in the world.

If you want to know Jesus and KNOW where you will spend eternity, get to a quiet place and ask Him to forgive you of all your sins and ask Him into your heart.

1 John 1:9 – If we confess our sins, he is faithful and just to forgive our sins and purify us from all unrighteousness.

Revelation 21:8 – But the cowardly, unbelieving, abominable, murderers, sexually immoral, sorcerers, idolaters, and all liars shall have their part in the lake which burns with fire and brimstone, which is the second death."

Jesus is God in flesh form. Jesus was born of a virgin. He died on a cross to save us from our sins. He led a perfect life to be the perfect sacrifice for you and me. He resurrected three days later to show His power over death! Jesus is the only way to Heaven. Time is short. Accept Jesus' offer of salvation today.

Admit to God that you are a sinner. Repent, turning away from your sin.

Romans 3:23 – For all have sinned, and come short of the glory of God.

Believe that Jesus is God's Son and accept God's gift of forgiveness from sin.
Romans 5:8 – While we were sinners, Christ died for us.

Confess your faith in Jesus Christ as your Savior and Lord.
Romans 10:9 – If you will confess with your mouth, "Jesus is Lord," and believe in your heart that God raised Him from the dead, you will be saved.

After a person admits to God that he or she is a sinner, repents and believes that Jesus is God's Son sent to die to pay for the sins of the world, and confesses that faith in Jesus, they are now a Christian and knows Jesus as their Savior.

Here is a prayer you can pray to God if you like, but this *must* be from your heart and you *mean* it. Remember, God looks at the heart and not anything external.

Dear God, thank You for choosing to love me! I know I am a sinner. I believe You sent Your Son, Jesus Christ, to die for my sins. I believe He rose again and lives today. Please forgive my sins, Lord. I turn away from my sin and I open the door of my heart and ask You to live in me. Thank You for Your wonderful love and for changing my life forever. In Jesus' name I pray, Amen.

If you said that prayer in earnest, you should feel differently. Start talking to Jesus as if He is right next to you – because He is! He will never leave you nor forsake you and He will stick closer than a brother. Not only that, but He will give you a peace that surpasses all understanding. Welcome to the family that will spend eternity together with our Lord and Savior, Jesus Christ. Hallelujah!

Philippians 2:10-11 – [10] That at the name of Jesus every knee should bow, of [things] in heaven, and [things] in earth, and [things] under the earth;

[11] And [that] every tongue should confess that Jesus Christ [is] Lord, to the glory of God the Father.

Ministries, Authors and Links:

To break curses, demonic strongholds and witchcraft:

Don Dickerman Ministries – www.dondickerman.com
Dr. Erica Shepherd – www.tedline.com
Dr. Pat Holliday – www.miracleinternetchurch.com
John Ramirez – www.johnramirez.org

YouTube Ministry Searches:

Pastor Charles Lawson
Henry Gruver
Ron Wyatt
Derek Prince
Barry R. Smith
Omegaman Radio
Leonard Ravenhill
Al Neal
Bill Wiese
Don Dickerman
Steve Quayle
Sid Roth
Mel Bond
Mark Taylor
Lord's Lessons

Recommended Authors:

Smith Wigglesworth
Lester Sumrall
Derek Prince
Kenneth Hagin
David Wilkerson
Barry R. Smith
Sadhu Sundar Singh
Watchman Nee
Mary K. Baxter
Roland Buck
Tom Horn
Ronnie Posey
Brother Lawrence
H. A. Baker
John Ramirez
David Flynn
Jackie Pullinger
Madam Guyon

For prayer: *karentokarse@gmail.com*

Made in the USA
Columbia, SC
12 March 2019